Contemporary Evangelism for the 21st Century

Carlton P. Byrd

Hardnett Publishing ©

Copyright © 2009 | Carlton P. Byrd
All rights reserved.

No part of this book may be reproduced or transmitted in any form or by any means, electronic or mechanical, including photocopying and recording, or by any information storage or retrieval system, except as may be expressly permitted in writing by the publisher.

ISBN 10: 0-9789310-8-4
ISBN 13: 978-0-9789310-8-7

Unless otherwise noted, Scripture quotations are from
The Holy Bible, King James Version

Printed in the United States of America

DEDICATION

This book is dedicated to my lovely wife, Danielle, and our three beautiful daughters, Caitlyn (deceased), Christyn, and Caileigh, whose unconditional love and support have enabled me to be an instrument in building the kingdom of God.

TABLE OF CONTENTS

Foreword	by Elder Vanard Mendinghall	vi
Chapter 1	INTRODUCTION	1
Chapter 2	A BIBLICAL AND THEOLOGICAL FOUNDATION OF EVANGELISM	9
Chapter 3	A BRIEF REVIEW OF CONTEMPORARY EVANGELISM	33
Chapter 4	HISTORICAL REVIEW OF TWENTIETH CENTURY SEVENTH DAY ADVENTIS EVANGELISTIC PRACTICES IN THE UNITED STATES	55
Chapter 5	DESIGN OF THE CONTEMPORARY EVANGELISM PLAN	77
Chapter 6	APPLICATION OF THE CONTEMPORARY EVANGELISM PLAN	103
Chapter 7	SUMMARY AND CONCLUSION	126

FOREWORD

I became familiar with the ministry of Dr. Carlton P. Byrd several years ago while he was pastoring the Maranatha Seventh-day Adventist Church in Tuscaloosa, Alabama. Even as a young minister, I found him to be a spiritual leader beyond his years. God has blessed him with vision, innovative thinking, and energy he so willingly spends for the mission of this church.

From its inception, evangelism has always been central to the growth of the Seventh-day Adventist Church. The attendance at Dr. Byrd's current church, Atlanta-Berean, quadrupled in a few short months after his arrival. With his ground-breaking approach to worship and evangelism together, it has been a catalyst for growth and change. As a result, we must continue to develop and embrace effective methods of reaching the unsaved. These contemporary approaches should demonstrate the relevance of the Seventh-day Adventist message to the issues of today and still adhere to the fundamental tenets of our faith.

In his book, *Contemporary Evangelism for the 21st Century*, Dr. Byrd has done just that. In this book, he carefully outlines the historical successes of evangelistic efforts of the Seventh-day Adventist Church. He goes on to provide a thoughtful, tested means of adapting the key elements of our prior successes to current day sociological realities.

This book is a must-read for any pastor, elder, deacon, Bible worker, or lay person in the Seventh-day Adventist Church who is sincere about our mission to introduce people to Jesus Christ and experience the joy of salvation.

- Elder Vanard Mendinghall, President
South Atlantic Conference of Seventh-day Adventists

CHAPTER 1

INTRODUCTION

"Our church is dying. We're stagnant. We're not growing. We need revival. We need to grow, and we want to grow. We need and want evangelism." These statements reflect the sentiments of numerous church members in the North American Division of the Seventh-day Adventist Church as cries for evangelism and church growth are plenteous. While total numerical membership in the Seventh-day Adventist Church in North America has steadily grown, the per capita number of new baptisms in recent years has not risen in proportion to this overall growth.[1]

The call for evangelism is not foreign or new to the Seventh-day Adventist Church. Since its formal organization in 1860, the Seventh-day Adventist Church, in harmony with its stated mission,[2] has fostered aggressive evangelistic endeavors throughout the world. Radio broadcasts, prophecy meetings, Bible study classes, tent revivals, hall meetings, and the like have all

---

[1] General Conference of Seventh-day Adventists, North American Division, Silver Spring, MD, Office of Statistics, 2008.

[2] *Seventh-day Adventist Church Manual* (Hagerstown, MD: Review and Herald Publishing Association, 2005), 90.

been conducted to facilitate church growth in harmony with the Holy Scriptures (Matt 28:18-20;[3] Acts 2:41, 47). Despite varied customs, cultures, and traditions reflected in our cosmopolitan, international society, worldwide membership of the Seventh-day Adventist Church has surpassed fifteen million members largely due to evangelistic efforts.[4]

Nevertheless, while worldwide membership for the Seventh-day Adventist Church is climbing, the growth rate for the North American Division which includes the United States, has shrunk in comparison to the other world divisions comprising the Seventh-day Adventist Church. In fact, the membership in the North American Division, the birthplace of Seventh-day Adventism, totals just over one million,[5] and while total Seventh-day Adventist Church membership in North America is increasing, this pace of growth has decreased when compared to the per capita growth as realized in former years.[6]

Because Seventh-day Adventists have a biblical mandate to evangelize (Matt 28:18-20; Rev 4:6, 7), the declining evangelistic effectiveness that is now being experienced in the United States

---

[4]General Conference of Seventh-day Adventists, Office of Statistics.

[5]Ibid.

[6]Russell Burrill, "Evangelism and Church Growth Syllabus," (Berrien Springs, MI: North American Division Evangelism Institute, 1994), 2.

needs to be addressed, particularly in our country's urban centers as nearly 90 percent of the nation's population resides in urban areas.[7] Additionally, ineffective evangelistic practices need to be abandoned, and consequently, modern evangelistic approaches employed to maximize church growth. Hence, the use of antiquated evangelistic methods must be changed and replaced by employing more relevant methodologies.

What are some of the reasons for this decline? Why has the Seventh-day Adventist Church become ineffective relative to evangelism in the United States? Do we understand the context to which we minister? Are we implementing evangelistic methodologies that are appropriate and relevant to the changing technological and socioeconomic conditions of American society in our postmodern world? Or are we merely performing "Eight Track Ministry in an MP3 Society?"

Before we move any further, I think it would be helpful for us to define specific terms that will be used in this book.

Definition of Terms

Postmodernism

---

[7]United States Census Bureau.

When referring to our postmodern society, this writer believes that Reinder Bruinsma, Seventh-day Adventist leader in the Netherlands, offers an adequate description of postmodernism. Bruinsma states:

> From the 1970s onward, the term postmodernism came into use to describe the changes that became more and more apparent in the arts and in architecture, and then also in philosophy and even theology. It cannot be denied that something is going on, particularly in the Western world. The Enlightenment era has come, or is rapidly coming to an end. We participate in a momentous process of change. The postmodern person does not believe that everything will become better and better. There are no absolutes. We all have our own private truths. The postmodern person has a strong dislike for religious institutions, but is open to spirituality. Religion is in, but the institutional church is out.[8]

This description, characterized by the lack of interest in the church's hierarchical structure, the growing disdain for centralized, institutional structures, the weariness of ecclesiastical authority, and lessened concern about church discipline, policy, or the church

---

[8] Reinder Bruinsma, "Modern Versus Postmodern Adventism: The Ultimate Divide?" *Ministry*, June 2005, 6-7.

manual, defines the postmodern Seventh-day Adventist.[9] While the number of postmodern Seventh-day Adventists is in the minority when compared to the majority of traditional Seventh-day Adventists, the former is a growing minority with emphasis on decentralization, experience, and expression. To address this growing postmodern mindset among many Seventh-day Adventists, an outlook that is a microcosm of the greater American Christian community, evangelistic methods as appropriate to current and future contexts are needed.

Contemporary

The terms, "current" and "future," carry a medley of connotations and can often be used interchangeably when referring to the relevancy of existing and impending time periods. The word "contemporary" is somewhat a blending of these two terms as it suggests present and imminent periods of time. Contemporary is a word derived from the Latin word, *comtempus* or *comtempor*, which means time.[10] Webster specifically defines contemporary as "living, occurring, or existing at the same time; of the same age; modern; current."[11]

---

[9]Ibid.

[10]Webster's Dictionary (1990), s.v. "Contemporary."

[11]Ibid.

Evangelism

Evangelism comes from the Greek word, *evangelion*, which means "good tidings."[12] Webster views evangelism succinctly as "preaching the gospel."[13] Renowned Church Growth Professor, Thom S. Rainer, defines evangelism as "the proclamation of the historical, biblical Christ as Savior and Lord, with a view to persuading people to come to Him personally and so be reconciled to God."[14] Former North American Division Ministerial Association Secretary (now retired), Russell Burrill, expounds even further on this definition and sees evangelism as "proclaiming Jesus Christ as God and Savior and persuading men to become His disciples and responsible members in His church."[15]

Contemporary Evangelism

In this book, contemporary evangelism will refer to evangelistic methodologies that are practiced in a manner relevant to current and future time periods. Put another way, contemporary evangelism is the proclamation of the gospel of Jesus Christ through relevant, applicable means to the current culture, context,

---

[12]Webster's Dictionary (1990), s.v. "Evangelism."

[13]Ibid.

[14]Thom S. Rainer, *The Book of Church Growth* (Nashville, TN: Broadman Press, 1993), 77-78.

[15]Burrill, 18.

and milieu in which we live with the view of winning individuals to Jesus Christ. Contemporary evangelism further envelops progressive evangelistic methods for the imminent future through proactive forecasting of societal trends, along with applicable implementation to them in our ever-evolving, postmodern culture.

In summation, if our mission as a church is the evangelization of the world, then our evangelistic methods must communicate the gospel of Jesus Christ to the specific constituency to which we minister while intentionally implementing evangelistic methodologies that are appropriate and relevant to our postmodern society. Therefore, as we seek to reach our highly secularized, socially diverse, and economically dissimulated culture, our methods of evangelism must change to reach the contemporary mind. Accordingly, that's what this book is about – fulfilling the mission of the Seventh-day Adventist Church in the United States through appropriate, relevant means. With that in mind, I welcome you to *Contemporary Evangelism for the Twenty-first Century*.

CHAPTER 2

A BIBLICAL AND THEOLOGICAL FOUNDATION OF EVANGELISM

Biblical Foundation of Evangelism

Seventh-day Adventists declare that the Bible is God's holy, inspired Word, the only rule of faith and practice for the Christian. They regard the Bible as the authentic, authoritative, infallible Word of God.[16] The Bible teaches that prior to the creation of this earth there was war in heaven between Christ (Michael) and Satan (the dragon). Christ was victorious in this war, and Satan was cast out of heaven into the earth. Satan's chief responsibility on the earth has been to deceive the world regarding the love of God (Rev 12:7-9).

Satan's deceptive activity began in the Garden of Eden with Adam and Eve. Despite implicit instructions from the Creator, earth's foreparents fell prey to Satan's cunning deceptions. Consequently, Adam and Eve's fall adversely affected

---

[16]General Conference of Seventh-day Adventists, Ministerial Association, *Seventh-day Adventists Believe...: A Biblical Exposition of 27 Fundamental Doctrines* (Hagerstown, MD: Review and Herald Publishing Association, 1988), 4.

God's entire creation. Since the fall of Adam and Eve, God has been "seeking" humanity in efforts to reconcile fallen creation. It was in the Garden of Eden after the fall that God asked Adam, "Where art thou?" (Gen 3:6, 9, 14-19). This question rests on the premise that the Creator desires to be involved in a seeking mission for fallen creation. Just as God sought Adam in the Garden of Eden, God is seeking fallen humanity today.

The heart of evangelism is in the heart of a seeking God. Throughout Old Testament Scripture, from God seeking Adam and Eve, to the Israelite exodus from Egypt by way of the Red Sea, to the saving of the Jewish nation as realized through the courage and resilience of Esther, God has desired to seek and save humanity (Gen 3; Exod 14; Esth 5-10). Because of the "seeking" and "saving" nature of God, the plan of redemption to restore humanity was fully effected in the New Testament as God sent His only begotten Son, Jesus Christ, so that through Jesus, humanity could have eternal life (John 3:16).

The Bible states, "In the beginning was the Word, and the Word was with God, and the Word was God. And the Word was made flesh, and dwelt among us, and we beheld His glory, the glory as of the only begotten of the Father, full of grace and truth" (John 1:1, 14). Hence, Jesus Christ, the Son of God, was not only active in creation, but was also active in re-creation and redemption through fulfilling the mission of God by being born of woman in human flesh and then dying on Calvary's cross for the remission of humanity's sins (John 1:29; 3:16, 17; Acts 4:12; Rev 12:11). The Son, just prior to His crucifixion, informed His disciples that He would send the Holy Spirit (Comforter) to lead them into all truth (John 14:16; 15:26). Furthermore, the Son left them with the gospel commission to tell a dying world that Jesus saves (Matt 28:9-20).

The church, established by Christ and the institution for which Christ sacrificed His life (Matt 16:18; Eph 5:25), is God's modern evangelistic agency by which God can reconcile and restore creation. The church, the body of Christ, is to join God in this seeking, missionary movement (Acts 2:41-47). The sending mission of Christ was to bring wholeness and healing to the world. The mission of the church is the same. The church has been sent by God to teach that healing comes through humanity's acceptance of Jesus Christ as Lord and Savior. The church in this "sending" is called out of the world, redeemed, and then sent back into the world to reach and transform the world.

Darrell Guder and Letty Russell share this sentiment and specifically refer to mission as "sending," expressing that this "sending" is the central biblical theme outlining the purpose of God's action in human history. The church is God's "sent people" to carry this gospel. Russell suggests that through this "sending," the church participates in God's mission in the redemption of humanity and the restoration of all creation. When understanding the mission of God and grasping the meaning of this "sending," she also proposes that one should envision God the Father sending the Son, and God the Father and the Son sending the Spirit. Furthermore, it should now be understood that the Father, Son, and the Holy Spirit are now sending the church into the entire world.[17]

Jesus' Approach to Evangelism

The mission of the Seventh-day Adventist Church is rooted in the Holy Scriptures as articulated by Jesus Christ in the great gospel commission, "Go ye therefore and teach all nations, baptizing them in the name of the Father, and of the Son, and of the Holy Ghost. Teaching them to observe all things whatsoever I have commanded you: and lo, I am with you always, even until the end of the world" (Matt 28:19, 20).

The gospel commission of Jesus Christ makes evangelism the primary function and duty of the church. The mission of the Seventh-day Adventist Church focuses on the prominence of

---

[17]Darrell Guder, ed., *Missional Church: A Vision for the Sending of the Church in North America* (Grand Rapids, MI: Eerdmans Publishing Association, 1998), 97; Letty Russell, *Church in the Round: Feminist Interpretation of the Church* (Louisville, KY: Westminster John Knox Press, 1993), 88.

evangelism throughout the entire world.[18] *Seventh-day Adventists Believe...: A Biblical Exposition of 27 Fundamental Doctrines*, a comprehensive explanation of Seventh-day Adventist doctrine, accentuates this point as follows, "The church is organized for mission service to fulfill the work Israel failed to do. As seen in the life of the Master, the greatest service the church provides the world is in being fully committed to completing the gospel 'witness to all nations' (Matt 24:14), empowered by the baptism of the Holy Spirit. This mission includes proclaiming a message of preparation for Christ's return that is directed both to the church itself and to the rest of humanity."[19]

The *Seventh-day Adventist Church Manual* further adds that the church board, composed of the principal officers of the church, has a number of important responsibilities, but "its chief concern is the spiritual nurture of the church and the work of planning and fostering evangelism in all its phases."[20]

Webster provides a theoretical definition of theology by stating it is "the study of the existence, nature, and laws of God."[21] Put practically, it is "confessing one's faith" in God. Douglas John

---

[18]*Seventh-day Adventist Church Manual*, 90.

[19]General Conference, *Seventh-day Adventists Believe*, 4.

[20]*Seventh-day Adventist Church Manual*, 90.

[21]Webster's Dictionary (1990), s.v. "Theology."

Hall states that to confess something is "to own, avow, declare, reveal, or disclose what in the depths of the soul one considers to truly be the case."[22] Seventh-day Adventists believe that the theological confession of the faith is the gospel commission of Jesus Christ. This commission rests in reaching the world through evangelism, the proclamation of the gospel.

Hall's interpretation of Christian confession implies worldly witness and public testimony. He emphasizes that the good news (gospel) by which Jesus Christ redeemed the world through His precious blood shed on Calvary must not be hoarded or confined, but rather it must be spread to all the earth.[23] The admonition to evangelize the entire world is inclusive of all believers in Christ, dating from the time of Christ's earthly life during His itinerant ministry until His Second Coming.

The apostle Paul verbalized the primacy of this witness and testimony when he expressed, "For I am not ashamed of the gospel of Christ: for it is the power of God unto salvation to every one that believeth" (Rom 1:16). Furthermore, the urgency in proclaiming the gospel is imperative for Jesus Himself said, "And this gospel of the kingdom shall be preached in all the world for a

---

[22]Douglas John Hall, *Confessing the Faith: Christian Theology in a North American Context* (Minneapolis, MN: Fortress Press, 1998), 8.

[23]Ibid., 147.

witness unto all nations; and then shall the end come" (Matt 24:14).

Christ's commission transcends national, cultural, racial, and economic lines. Disciples are to be made of all people with no respect to background (Acts 1:8; Gal 3:26-29). The call to evangelism is universal and ubiquitous. The church is to be a missionary church in the cultures where its residence is held. The church is not the mission or goal of the gospel, but its instrument and witness. Church growth expert, C. Peter Wagner, concurs in the following statement that "Christian mission is what God sends us to do. He sends us out as ambassadors of His kingdom into a world yet dominated by the evil one. The heart of the Gospel Commission is to make disciples of all nations. In light of the kingdom of God, each person who becomes a disciple of Jesus Christ is another person lost to the dominion of Satan."[24]

Christians, which by their very name are implicated as disciples or followers of Christ, have been called by God to carry this gospel to humanity; to exercise the "confession" of the faith. The church is to be that community which is being brought to live the representative life of Christ in this world.[25] To represent the life of Christ is to portray and stand for what He espoused when on

---

[24]C. Peter Wagner, *Your Church Can Be Healthy* (Nashville, TN: Abingdon Press, 1979), 33.

[25]Hall, 45.

this earth. So although the work of the incarnate Christ on this earth is finished, the church's participation in this work as Christ's representative is not. The entire church is to commit itself to the commissioning of the gospel. As Jesus made disciples of individuals, the church must also seek to proclaim the gospel message to others, and make disciples to proclaim the gospel message of Christ.

Throughout the New Testament, followers of Christ are challenged to be a "sending" people and to evangelize. Christ exhorts His people to let their lights shine (Matt 5:16). He also challenges them to preach the gospel to every creature (Mark 16:1). He then expresses that His disciples are His witnesses (Luke 24:28). In the parable of the Lost Sheep, Jesus teaches the importance of every shepherd seeking that one lost sheep, even if he has to leave the ninety-nine in the wilderness. "What man of you, having an hundred sheep, if he lose one of them, doth not leave the ninety and nine in the wilderness, and go after that which is lost, until he find it?" (Luke 15:4).

God's urgent, eschatological message calls for the people of God to take the everlasting gospel to all the inhabitants of the earth, calling for them to fear and worship God who made the heavens, earth, seas, and fountains of water (Rev 14:6, 7). The fact that the message of the first angel of Rev 14 indicates an "everlasting gospel" should not be read casually. Rather, the insertion of the word, "everlasting," emphasizes the distinction that this gospel is the only gospel that can save humanity. The acceptance of this gospel will lead to loyalty and allegiance to God.

When Jesus commissioned His disciples to preach the gospel to every creature (Mark 16:15), to His small group of followers this task seemed like an impossible assignment until they understood His plan for its fulfillment. Christ's plan is so outlined, "When He ascended up on high, He led captivity captive, and gave gifts unto men. And He gave some, apostles; and some, prophets; and some, evangelists; and some, pastors and teachers; for the perfecting of the saints, for the word of the ministry for the edifying of the body of Christ" (Eph 4:7, 11-12). Put simply, the church is composed of followers who have been equipped with diverse gifts to share the mission of Jesus Christ, which is the evangelization of the world.

Jesus Christ advocated and practiced relevant evangelism when on this earth, while modeling a people-oriented, relational focus. He never de-valued the importance of people and their needs. "Christ's method alone will give true success in reaching people. The Savior mingled with men as one who desired their good. He showed His sympathy for them, ministered to their needs, and won their confidence. Then He bade them, 'Follow me.'"[26] Christ's method was neither contentious, argumentative, nor irrelevant. Christ approached individuals in loving service, and met their human needs in an appropriate, humane fashion.

Through His relational approach to ministry, Jesus contextualized His evangelistic methods to the cultures and age to which He found Himself. He reached people at their diverse levels of need, and then He shared the "good news" with them. As a result, they were receptive to His teachings and message. If the church is to effectively evangelize the world, then it must be able to identify with the current and future social, as well as spiritual, needs of society.

Jesus' method of evangelism is illustrated in John 4:1-42. Jesus met the woman at the well and asked her for a drink. He began socially conversing with her, and remained positive with her without condemning her. After winning her confidence, He then confronted her with the gospel with the statement, "I that speak unto thee am the Christ" (John 4:26).

Like Christ, the church must contact others through relevant, friendly relationships. We cannot win individuals to Jesus Christ if we are isolated, insulated, and not a "seeking" people. The church has been sent by God "to seek." Church

---

[26]Ellen G. White, *Ministry of Healing* (Boise, ID: Pacific Press Publishing Association, 1905), 143.

members need to establish common interests with unchurched individuals, arouse that interest, gain the respective individual's confidence, and avoid judgment or condemnation. Ultimately, the unchurched should be confronted with the gospel of Jesus Christ.

Guder teaches that the church needs to set as its foundation "the reign of God." This reign of God is rooted in God's mission to reconcile God's creation through the accomplished death and resurrection of Jesus.[27] The gospel, in essence, is Jesus Christ Himself. He became the incarnate Son of God to save us all from sin and death. Therefore, if the church is to receive and enter this reign of God, it will decide to turn from other hopes and loyalties, while seeking to accumulate a singular hope in one true God.

If the entire church would receive and enter the reign of God, Guder suggests that three things would happen. For one, evangelism would move from an act of recruiting with those outside the church to an invitation of companionship. Secondly, the community of the church would testify that they have the announcement that such a reign is coming, and indeed is already loose in the world. Finally, to those invited, the church would offer itself to assist their entrance into the reign of God and travel with them as co-pilgrims.[28]

---

[27]Guder, 97-98.

[28]Ibid.

The Writings of Ellen G. White

Seventh-day Adventists believe that Ellen G. White was an inspired prophetess,[29] and her writings are more revered and popular than any other Seventh-day Adventist writer. A founding member of the Seventh-day Adventist Church in the mid-nineteenth century, she too, had much to say about the evangelization of the world. Her writings on evangelism are so extensive that there are over 275 references to evangelism listed in the *Comprehensive Index to the Writings of Ellen G. White*. In fact, many of these selected writings were compiled upon permission from the trustees of her estate, and published into the book entitled, *Evangelism*.

Throughout the book, *Evangelism*, and in numerous other works, Mrs. White promotes and fosters the need for evangelism in our world. Although she addresses diverse evangelistic issues in varying cultural and societal contexts ranging from appropriate versus inappropriate evangelistic styles to the funding for evangelistic campaigns, she consistently stresses in her writings that evangelism is the primary work of the Seventh-day Adventist Church. She asserts that "the God-given work of Seventh-day

---

[29]General Conference, *Seventh-day Adventists Believe*, 216, 224-226.

Adventists is the evangelization of the world."[30] In *Christian Service*, she adds, "The church must realize its obligation to carry the gospel of present truth to every creature."[31]

Mrs. White clearly advocated the biblical mandate for the Seventh-day Adventist Church to engage in the work of evangelism. She states, "We are not, as Christians, doing 1/20 the part that we might do in winning souls to Christ. There is a world to be warned, and every sincere Christian will be a guide and an example to others in faithfulness, in cross-bearing, in prompt and vigorous action, in unswerving fidelity to the cause of truth, and in sacrifices and labors to promote the cause of God."[32]

Her support of this biblical mandate for evangelism is exemplified in her full adherence of the gospel commission that Christ gave His disciples just prior to His heavenly ascension in Matt 28:19, 20. She, however, makes the commission specifically applicable to Christ's disciples today. She says, "To us also the commission is given. We are bidden to go forth as Christ's messengers, to teach, instruct, and persuade men and women, to urge upon their attention the word of life. And to us also the

---

[30]Ellen G. White, *Gospel Workers* (Washington, DC: Review and Herald Publishing Association, 1948), 57.

[31]Ellen G. White, *Christian Service* (Takoma Park, MD: Home Missionary Department of the General Conference of Seventh-day Adventists, 1947), 80.

[32]Ibid., 257.

assurance of Christ's abiding presence is given. Whatever the difficulties with which we may have to contend, whatever the trials we may have to endure, the gracious promise is always ours. 'Lo, I am with you always, even unto the end of the world.'"[33]

Mrs. White promoted evangelism and her lifetime was spent formulating methods of reaching the unreached. Her history shows that she traveled extensively sharing the gospel, published comprehensive evangelistic material, and taught workers within the Seventh-day Adventist Church on effective modes of evangelism while stressing the importance of intentional, continual engagement in evangelism. "Evangelistic work, opening the Scriptures to others, warning men and women of what is coming upon the world is to occupy more and still more of the time of God's servants. If every Seventh-day Adventist had done the work laid upon him, the number of believers would now be much larger than it is."[34]

Significance of Evangelism to Church Vitality

While the word "evangelism" has been given many different definitions and descriptions, some of which were shared

---

[33] Ibid., *Evangelism* (Washington, DC: Review and Herald Publishing Association, 1946), 15.

[34] Ibid., 17.

previously in this book, evangelism has often been coined metaphorically as the "life-blood" of the church. All affirmative church activity, movement, and operation exist and stem from evangelistic endeavors. The consistent influx of new members, coupled with the energy and enthusiasm that church growth brings, attribute to the life, vivacity, and positive spirit of the church.

There is a sense of joy and excitement when new members are added to the membership of the church. Positive, supportive attitudes are apparent within evangelism-driven churches. Members have a high level of enthusiasm for participation within the church. Lethargic, slothful attitudes are not as widespread when evangelism is apparent among parson and parishioners. When active evangelism is absent within a church, the church spirit is often dead, with the church headed for disintegration. Russell Burrill describes disintegration as the stage within the life cycle of a church where morale among the members is very low and the primary goal of the church becomes preservation and survival.[35]

Evangelism also keeps the members of the church active in church affairs. Most importantly, members are more cognizant of the church's mission when evangelism is continually practiced by the membership. Ellen White says that "an idle mind is Satan's

---

[35]Burrill, "Evangelism and Church Growth," 84-85.

workshop."[36] She adds, "Vigilance and fidelity have been required of Christ's followers in every age; but now that we are standing upon the very verge of the eternal world, holding the truths we do, having so great light, so important a work, we must double our diligence. Every one is to do the very utmost of his ability. My brother, you endanger your own salvation if you hold back now. God will call you to account if you fail in the work He has assigned you."[37]

Moreover, the probability of members actively working in the cause of God increases the likelihood of their being fortified with personal spiritual growth. George Knowles in his book, *How to Help Your Church Grow*, says, "When we who claim to be God's people move out in obedient service for Him, we become more aware of our spiritual needs. At the same time, we qualify for a greater infilling of the Holy Spirit, which is given for service."[38]

Christians become like Christ as they share in His work. This is the basic reason God has shared with us the privilege of service. Mrs. White expresses, "God could have reached His

---

[36]White, *Education* (Boise, ID: Pacific Press Publishing Association, 1903), 190.

[37]White, *Christian Service*, 79.

[38]George E. Knowles, *How to Help Your Church Grow* (Hagerstown, MD: Review and Herald Publishing Association, 1997), 144.

objective in saving sinners without our aid; but in order for us to develop a character like Christ's, we must share in His work."[39] So although God does not need the church and can communicate His message and do His work without human vessels, the church needs involvement with God in service.

When the church lessens its outward, missionary focus, members begin to center their attentions on internal matters. They lose sight of the gospel commission, and evangelistic opportunities and endeavors become foreign. The *Seventh-day Adventist Church Manual* clearly states, "When the church board devotes its first interests and highest energies to every-member evangelism, most church problems are alleviated or prevented. A strong, positive influence is felt in the spiritual life and growth of the membership."[40]

To the contrary, when church members begin focusing on their personal needs as opposed to concentrating on the needs of the church and community, "koinonitis" develops. "Koinonitis, " by definition, is "when interpersonal relationships within the church become so central, that they become the focal point for almost all church activity and involvement."[41] As a result, the

---

[39]White, *Christian Service*, 8.

[40]*Seventh-day Adventist Church Manual*, 90.

[41]Burrill, "Evangelism and Church Growth," 14.

overall spiritual growth of the church is lessened and evangelistic activity is minimal.

When the church fails to engage in evangelism, its purpose is often lost and mission misunderstood. Evangelism keeps the church rooted in its mission. People working for the salvation of souls are not plagued with unnecessary strife. The spirituality of the church collectively, as well as personally, is strengthened through the constructive work of evangelism.

To further comprehend the impact evangelism imparts to the vitality of a church, one must recognize that a fuller understanding of evangelism would exist with a greater explanation given to the denotation of a disciple in relationship to evangelism. While evangelism rests in proclaiming Jesus Christ as Lord and Savior, and should be the focus of the entire church membership, convincing individuals to also become His disciples should accompany the former. This promotes the concept that "each one, should reach one."

As individuals become disciples of Christ, they are very apt to see others become disciples of Christ too. A simplistic definition of a disciple is a "follower."[42] First and foremost, to become a disciple or follower of Christ, one must be willing to repudiate self. Individuals have to be at God's bidding in their

---

[42]Webster's Dictionary (1990), s.v. "Disciple."

respective lives. Jesus Christ expressed that those who are desirous of following Him, must be willing to deny themselves, and take up their cross in order to follow Him (Mark 8:34). True evangelism is a process that incorporates this self-renouncement and pursues the path of God's will.

Yet, to become a disciple of Christ, one must also understand that there should be a yearning to make others disciples as well. This is what Christ meant when He said, "Go ye therefore and teach all nations baptizing them in the name of the Father, and of the Son, and of the Holy Spirit. Teaching them to observe all things whatsoever I have commanded you" (Matt 28:19-20).

Although evangelism is defined as "preaching the gospel,"[43] it is not restricted to one's conviction that Jesus Christ is Lord, or just simply to be a "follower" of Christ. It continues with instruction and teaching on the part of the current and prospective disciple. Donald McGavran's twofold understanding of church growth is "discipling," which is the initial coming to Christ, and the "perfecting," the full instruction into the Christian faith.[44] "Without the exercise of the mental faculties to understand the revealed will of God, there can be no real Christianity, no real

---

[43]Webster's Dictionary (1990), s.v. "Evangelism."

[44]Donald McGavran, quoted in Russell Burrill, class notes from Evangelism and Church Growth, Seventh-day Adventist Theological Seminary, Andrews University, Berrien Springs, MI, Fall Quarter, 1994, 17, photocopied.

growth. Instruction is thus of vital importance before and after baptism."[45]

Finally, a disciple of Christ is one who has fellowship with other disciples. Acts 2:41-42 teaches that after individuals were persuaded and convinced that Jesus Christ was indeed the Savior, they aspired to fellowship with other disciples of Christ. Evangelism is accepting Christ, becoming a disciple of Christ, following Christ, sharing Christ, and then fellowshipping with others in Christ.

True Christians will engage in evangelism each and everyday. They will not confine evangelism to a limited day, or season. Effective discipling means everyday evangelism. Emphasizing not only the denial of self, but also daily evangelism, Jesus said in Luke 9:23, "If any man will come after me, let him deny himself, and take up his cross daily and follow me." When one really studies the Bible, the student of the Word is convinced that evangelism was the main function of the early church, and not a matter of secondary importance. The New Testament Church followed the command of Jesus so completely that "daily in the temple, and in every house, they ceased not to teach and preach Jesus Christ" (Acts 5:42). They were so anxious to do God's will

---

[45]"Matthew," *SDA Bible Commentary*, ed. F. Nichol (Washington, DC: Review and Herald Publishing Association, 1980), 5:557.

they went "praising God and having favor with all the people until the Lord added daily as such should be saved" (Acts 2:47). Because they had undertaken this great burden for lost souls, the Lord added three thousand new converts to the church (Acts 2:41).

As the apostles were Christ's witnesses then, we are His witnesses now. The work that God began through them, God will finish through the church as it demonstrates by total dedication that the church is God's modern day witness. Paul magnifies this concept by saying, "I beseech you therefore, brethren, by the mercies of God, that ye present your bodies a living sacrifice, holy, acceptable unto God, which is your reasonable service. And be not conformed to this world: but be ye transformed by the renewing of your mind, that ye may prove what is that good, and acceptable, and perfect, will of God" (Rom 12:1-2).

Gottfried Oosterwal, in his book, *Mission Impossible*, reminds us that "though the Lord has never told us that the whole world will accept Him, He did definitely commission us to proclaim the gospel to every person on earth. Since Christ died for all of them, they have a right to know it. Therein lies the challenge of our generation.[46] Therefore, while we can't save anybody (Holy Spirit's role), we can tell everybody.

---

[46]Gottfried Oosterwal, *Mission Possible* (Nashville, TN: Southern Publishing Association, 1972), quoted in George E. Knowles, *How to Help Your Church Grow* (Hagerstown, MD: Review and Herald, 1997), 44.

"The church's main emphasis must be winning lost souls for Jesus Christ. We must do everything in our churches for the glory of God. We must realize that heaven does not shout over financial rallies or singing programs, but over the church's burden to win lost souls."[47] Jesus said, "I say unto you, that likewise joy shall be in heaven over one sinner that repenteth, more than over ninety and nine just persons, which need no repentance" (Luke 15:7).

Churches actively involved in evangelism experience spiritual revival. The New Testament Church of Acts 2 grew because it had an internal spiritual revival. There was a sense of centrality within the mission. Everyone knew their reason for existence, the proclamation of the gospel. When evangelism is paramount within a church, churches are strengthened spiritually given the necessary increased Bible study among members in preparation for this gospel proclamation. Evangelism keeps individuals rooted in the Word of God. Both the disciple of Christ, as well as the prospective disciple, benefit from the effects of evangelism. Both read the Word, study the Word, and experience the outpouring of the Holy Spirit through the proclamation of the

---

[47]J. Herbert Hinkle, *Soul Winning in Black Churches* (Grand Rapids, MI: Baker Book House, 1973), 104.

Word. When this is accomplished, the power of God will be seen, felt, and heard throughout the church individually and collectively.

CHAPTER 3

A BRIEF REVIEW OF CONTEMPORARY EVANGELISM

Introduction

The enthusiasm and expectancy surrounding the year 2000, and ultimately, the turn of this new year, decade, century, and millennium, captured the world's attention as no other date. The end of the twentieth century and the beginning of the twenty-first century gave common theme and title to magazines, books, television and radio shows, New Age optimism, and apocalyptic pessimism. For some, it was just another date. For others, it symbolized the end of one era and the beginning of another. For the latter, this date symbolized not only specific changes, but also change itself.

When considering this notion of change, I would dare to suggest that more societal changes have occurred in the past 100 years than in the previous 2,000 years. To further magnify this concept, I would even argue that the changes in the final ten years of the twentieth century doubtlessly exceeded the changes of the first ninety years of the same century. It is not that change is new, but the rate of change in our world is unprecedented given society's technological and industrial advances.

In harmony with society's general resistance to change, some Christians, including Seventh-day Adventists, prefer to ignore these changes. Tragically, they continue to minister in the twenty-first century with methods that were used effectively in the twentieth century, which has resulted in many active church memberships declining or increasing, but only at a negatively accelerated rate. Therefore, ignoring the reality that changes exist will not stop change.

Evangelistic methodologies are not immune to this change. "Tent revivals have been replaced by stadium crusades. Televangelists are no longer limited to network broadcasting, but have now moved to satellite feeds that reach every nation in the world. Faithful "mom and pop" Christian bookstores are closing by the hundreds because Christian publishers are now placing their products in the "big" retailers, including Wal-Mart, Costco, Target, and Barnes & Noble."[48] Otis B. Moss, III, acknowledges this change and expresses, "There is a paradigm shift moving across the ecclesiastical landscape of America. If we miss this shift, our churches will be nothing more than boasting apparitions of what could have been and should have been. That thing you were

---

[48]George Barna, *Revolution* (Carol Stream, IL: Tyndale House Publishers, 2005), 10.

holding on to – that was then, but God is doing something in the now."[49]

Numerous other writers on the state of the church universal in the United States, some of which are shared in this chapter, underscore that this shift is present necessitating a call for change in the church's evangelistic methodologies. Hence, according to Christopher C. Mathis, Jr., "the church is challenged with the responsibility of making its programs and ministries culturally and contemporarily relevant to real-life needs and issues."[50]

When referring to the need for these changes in evangelism, one of America's most renowned church growth authors, George Barna, specifically states: "Change is a natural, positive, and irreplaceable part of growth. Leaders often remind us that what got us where we are is not the same stuff that will get us where we want to go, so we must change. Psychologists remind us that repeating the same behaviors merely generates the same outcomes, and therefore precludes rather than produces positive

---

[49]Otis B. Moss, III, "That Was Then, This is Now," *The African American Pulpit* (Hope for Life International, Inc. 10, no. 1, (Winter, 2006-07): 7.

[50]Christopher C. Mathis, Jr., "Evangelizing and Discipling Youth and College Students," in *Evangelism and Discipleship in African-American Churches*, ed. Lee June (Grand Rapids, MI: Zondervan Publishing House, 1999), 143.

change. In other words, to grow, we must purposefully alter our routines and approaches."[51]

Donald C. Posterski, another church growth writer, also supports the concept that our evangelistic methodologies must change. He states, "Our old strategies to reach others with the gospel, for the most part, simply no longer work. And just as Jesus understood the culture He was trying to reach and tailored His message to it, so too, we must understand our times and adjust our strategies accordingly."[52]

Two Major Societal Developments Affecting Need for Contemporary Evangelism

Postmodernism

Numerous reasons can be offered for the triggering of the aforementioned shift that is taking place in American Christianity, ranging from the increased information age to scientific and technological advances. Nevertheless, I would like to highlight two major influences that have had an enormous impact on society and have become hindrances to traditional evangelistic modalities

---

[51] Barna, 41.

[52] Donald C. Posterski, *Reinventing Evangelism* (Downers Grove, IL: InterVarsity Press, 1989), 14.

as used in former years affecting the need for contemporary evangelism. The first societal development, as cited in Reinder Bruinsma's description in Chapter 1, is the rise of postmodernism.

As many church growth writers suggest, we currently live in a contemporary society of growing postmodernists, particularly Baby Busters (those born from 1965 through 1983) and Mosaics (those born from 1984 to 2002) that claim there are "no moral absolutes."[53] In short, these postmodernists subscribe to the belief that truth is whatever you believe it to be, and that we are to become tolerant of all viewpoints, behavioral preferences, and styles of living. Such a mindset that fosters an "anything goes" philosophy is of major significance to Seventh-day Adventist evangelism because it is in direct conflict with Seventh-day Adventist theology which espouses biblical truths as the only rule of faith and practice for the Christian.[54]

Bruinsma offers a very detailed depiction of the postmodernist mindset that is a growing minority in Western culture with the following statement, "The postmodern person has a strong dislike for religious institutions, but is open to spirituality. Experience and emotion are okay, but doctrines are considered largely irrelevant. Absolute, propositional truth is replaced by

---

[53] Barna, 44.

[54] *Seventh-day Adventist Church Manual*, 32.

'what works for me,' and there are as many legitimate ways to interpret the Bible as there are readers. Sin has been reduced to a sense of regret that things have not gone as expected, with little or no place for something like atonement, where Someone steps in on my behalf."[55]

He also says that postmodernists acknowledge that worship styles have changed, and desire an increasing emphasis on experience, contemporary music, drama, and informal small group meetings. They think and act locally and have little or no interest in church hierarchy and are suspicious of centralized institutional structures.[56] Again, this contradicts traditional Seventh-day Adventist polity which possesses five levels of hierarchal structure in the United States as identified by the General Conference, North American Division, union conference, local conference, and local church.[57]

This emerging postmodern ideology further insists that one's values are based on one's individual tastes. Lesslie

---

[55]Bruinsma, 3.

[56]Ibid., 3-4.

[57]General Conference of Seventh-day Adventists, Office of Archives and Statistics, *2006 Yearbook of the Seventh-day Adventist Church* (Hagerstown, MD: Review and Herald Publishing Association, 2006), 19-20, 159-218.

Newbigin declares that "value systems embodied in styles of living are not right or wrong, true or false. They are matters of personal choice. The operative principle is respect for the freedom of each person to choose the values that he or she will live by."[58] Therefore, if one is judgmental, he or she breaks the social code as personal ethics has an elastic quality that can be stretched, and as long as one's conduct does not violate social standards or the criminal code, one is alright.[59] Relative to values, Posterski adds that "moral decisions, ethical dilemmas, and lifestyle options are now areas where we must make a myriad of decisions. The culture no longer hands down an accepted set of rules for how to live or provides a single standard for judging right and wrong."[60] Hence, each individual determines the correctness of his or her beliefs, thoughts, and actions.

Because of this emphasis on individual values and freedom, many church growth writers contend that religious organizations which demonstrate inclusiveness, as opposed to exclusivity, will grab the allegiance of postmodernists over those organizations that are perceived to be narrow or judgmental. In fact, postmodernists shy away from centralized religious structures or organizations

---

[58]Lesslie Newbigin, *Foolishness to the Greeks* (Grand Rapids, MI: William B. Eerdsmans Publishing Co., 1986), 17.

[59]Posterski, 67.

[60]Ibid., 64.

given their narrow, "one-size-fits all" philosophy. For them, "pressing the point that there is only way one to God goes too far."[61] Seventh-day Adventists, on the other hand, subscribe to the biblical injunction that "straight is the gate, and narrow is the way which leadeth unto (eternal) life" (Matt 7:14).

Postmodernists "have no use for churches that play religious games, whether those games are worship services that drone on without the presence of God or ministry programs that bear no spiritual fruit."[62] The younger, postmodernist mindset questions the relevance of these organizations and institutions, and believes that they serve as inhibitions to their quest for spiritual growth and expression. Barna states, "The pet peeve of the younger generations is irrelevance. They quickly abandon anything that is not wholly germane to their personal passions. They have little patience for anything based on tradition, customs, ease, or social acceptability. If they do not immediately sense the relevance of something, they dismiss it out of hand and move on to the next alterative."[63]

Lastly, postmodernists believe that morality is a private matter and relationships are more important than religion. Barna

---

[61] Ibid., 67.

[62] Barna, 13.

[63] Ibid.

offers, "There is more enthusiasm for creating personal dialogue with non-Christian friends than for bringing them to a big evangelistic event."[64] Such a philosophy definitely presents challenges to the traditional practices of Adventist public evangelism which promotes inviting and bringing individuals to corporate evangelistic programs including church revivals, tent crusades, and prophecy series meetings.

Because of the relationship emphasis of postmodernism, Barna proposes that by 2025, the spiritual profile of America will be dramatically different as he estimates that only about one-third of the nation's population will depend upon a local congregation as the primary or exclusive means for experiencing their faith. Consider Barna's forecast on how Americans will experience and express their faith as listed in Table 1.

TABLE 1

HOW AMERICANS EXPERIENCE AND EXPRESS THEIR FAITH[65]

	Local Church	Alternative Faith-Based Community	Family	Media, Arts, & Culture
2000	70%	5%	5%	20%
2025	30-35%	30-35%	5%	30-35%

---

[64]Ibid., 46-47.

[65]Ibid., 49.

Given postmodernists' emphasis on relevance and relationships, coupled with their desire to freely express their faith in new, non traditional ways, the current challenge to share the gospel of Jesus utilizing innovative, appropriate methods is great. Therefore, Poterski calls for a "re-invention" of our evangelistic strategies and summarizes the mandate to reach this contemporary, postmodern culture in the following assertion:

> Language about God is approaching obsolescence, being relegated to funerals and other official ceremonies that are still deemed necessary. If the world is going to hear God's good news, it needs to be repackaged. His eternal truth needs to be tuned to the times and communicated in concepts that connect with people in today's world. Some words get overused. Christian clichés and the reiteration of religious rhetoric literally drains life out of life-giving ideas. Christian preaching adds to the lament when it is more boring than intriguing. Lack of imagination from preachers, or perhaps it is an inordinate concern to appear orthodox, converts the good news into old news. When you've heard it before, what's the point in listening to it again?[66]

Ultimately, societal thinking is very different today than it was in former years, and the impact of this postmodernism is very

---

[66]Posterski, 95-96.

prevalent. "All generations do not think alike. Individuals born before World War II are more likely to think deductively and systematically and to have a deferred gratification ethic. 'Baby busters' (those born after 1964), however, more typically think inductively and eclectically and have an instant gratification ethic."[67] To be effective with persons of our postmodern generation will require an increase in "inductive reasoning and communication, an issue-by-issue customized approach to needs and questions, and an emphasis on the present power of the gospel of Jesus Christ."[68]

Urban Growth

A second major development necessitating the employment of contemporary evangelism is the increased growth of urban centers in the United States. An empirical study on population trends and analysis states that most American residents are significantly populated in our metropolitan areas. "In the United States, migration from rural to urban areas has been continuous. In 1920, about half the population lived in rural areas. By 1950, the number living on farms dropped to 15 percent. Now it is less than two percent. The United States has become an urban and suburban

---

[67]Leith Anderson, "The Church at History's Hinge," *Argos Ministries: Bibliotheca Sacra*, 151, (January–March, 1994): 10.

[68]Ibid.

society with ninety-eight percent of its population residing in cities."[69] In fact, according to the United States Census Bureau, nearly ninety percent of American residents currently reside in metropolitan areas of 100,000 persons or more, up from fifty-six percent in 1950.[70]

Ray Bakke, in the book *Planting and Growing Urban Churches: From Dream to Reality*, writes a chapter entitled, "The Challenge of World Evangelization to Mission Strategy," where he clearly expresses that evangelicals "cannot escape world urbanization." He says, "Over two billion people live in cities and the number grows much faster than in rural areas worldwide. The people who sought to flee Chicago have bumped into the people who fled Los Angeles. There is no place to hide. It is absolutely critical that we consider the implications of such explosive urbanization for evangelism."[71]

"The Adventist message and mission began in the horse-and-buggy era when almost everyone lived in rural villages and

---

[69] William D. Perreault, Jr. and E. Jerome McCarthy, *Essentials of Marketing*, 8th ed. (Boston, MA: Irwin McGraw-Hill, 2000), 93.

[70] United States Census Bureau.

[71] Ray Bakke, "The Challenge of World Evangelization to Mission Strategy," in *Planting and Growing Urban Churches: From Dream to Reality*, ed. Harvie M. Conn (Grand Rapids, MI: Baker Books, 1997), 83.

work centered around farming. Today it speaks to a world where most people reside in cities and life is driven by science and technology."[72] Therefore, the evangelistic methods that were formerly successful and complemented the rural nature of society are diminishing in effectiveness when seeking to captivate urban lifestyle. This urban lifestyle, characterized by two wage earning incomes among married couples, the rise of single parent homes, decreased opportunity for leisure, the expansion of suburban areas, rising crime, and inner-city poverty, impedes evangelistic practices that require availability and accessibility.

"Urban Ministry," as Bakke sees it, "is not so much a set of evangelistic techniques as it is a whole new way of envisioning the world about us."[73] With this in mind, new evangelistic strategies are needed to deal with the realism of urbanization. Consequently, because of increased urban growth, the expectations, anticipation, and appeal associated with church ministry, and evangelism in particular, are totally different today.

Church growth writer and demographer, James E. Westgate, stresses that the "strategies for these world-class cities will need to cope with the intense pressures created by a

---

[72]Monte Sahlin, *Adventist Congregations Today* (Lincoln, NE: Center for Creative Ministry, 2003), 71.

[73]Ibid., 88.

multiplicity of cultures, languages, classes, religions, and political structures."[74] Westgate contends that for evangelistic methods to be successful in our contemporary society, they should be all inclusive and meet the needs of everyone. Churches, he says, "must meet all the needs of the urban family," reaching the "up-and-outer as well as the down-and-outer."[75]

Contemporary Evangelism and Seventh-day Adventists

Given the changing theoretical outlook within American culture regarding spirituality as reflected in postmodernism and urban growth, the Seventh-day Adventist Church will have to alter its evangelistic practices to more effectively reach society. Contemporary evangelism, as defined in Chapter One, whether willingly or reluctantly, will have to be embraced.

Monte Sahlin, in *Adventist Congregations Today*, a comprehensive study about the state of the Seventh-day Adventist Church in America at the beginning of the twenty-first century, reminds us that "seven generations have been born since the

---

[74]James E. Westgate, "Church-Planting Strategies for World-Class Cities," in *Planting and Growing Urban Churches: From Dream to Reality*, ed. Harvie M. Conn (Grand Rapids, MI: Baker Books, 1997), 204.

[75]Ibid., 210.

Seventh-day Adventist Church emerged in the 1850s from the aftermath of the Millerite movement and the 'Great Disappointment.' The Seventh-day Adventist Church has now become a global faith with organizations in almost every country listed by the United Nations."[76] Yet, Sahlin says that "the Adventist Church does not seem to yet be at the tipping point where it boldly claims its future. For every member who sees his or her local church moving in a new direction, there are three who are still thinking about it, holding on to the past, or in despair."[77]

Nevertheless, every generation of Christians faces a new viewpoint in the world, which means that new strategies and methods are needed to interface with and influence the community around it. Renowned Seventh-day Adventist evangelist, Mark Finley, says, "Many contemporary unchurched people believe the church is not relevant. It has not kept up with the changing world. Secular people have a feeling of boredom and detachment during religious services."[78] While this feeling is prevalent among persons who visit churches in general, Ron Gladden suggests that this feeling is also present internally among many Seventh-day Adventists. He says, "Society has changed. The Baby Boomers

---

[76]Sahlin, 71.

[77]Ibid., 78.

[78]Mark A. Finley, "Secularism: Then and Now," *Ministry*, June, 2001, 7.

are no longer bringing their kids to church, and the generation that has followed is not bringing their kids to church either."[79]

So although principles are continual, practices do change and correspond to varying contexts and eras. With this in mind, Gottfried Oosterwal maintains that there is nothing sacred about evangelistic forms and structures. They are only "temporary-necessary," but temporary means to a goal. The only real criterion is whether they enable us to engage with the world of our time in the evangelistic outreach of the church.[80]

To expand the call for additional innovative evangelistic methodologies, Sahlin expresses that community involvement and visibility are key issues for church growth in the Seventh-day Adventist Church. According to Sahlin, the growing Seventh-day Adventist churches are those, among other things, with significant, non-traditional community services and active relationships with the neighborhood.[81] He adds that for Seventh-day Adventists, the

---

[79]Ron Gladden, *The Seven Habits of Highly Ineffective Churches* (Lincoln, NE: Advent Source, 2003), 58.

[80]Gottfried Oosterwal, *Mission Possible*, quoted in David M. Parks, "A Design for Contemporary Public Evangelism in the Upper Columbia Conference," (D.Min. dissertation, SDA Theological Seminary, Andrews University, 1987), 19-20.

[81]Sahlin, 19.

"most effective way to do public evangelism is through the worship service on Sabbath."[82]

It should be known that the community service activities Sahlin refers to that promote church growth are not the traditional activities of "community services" as predominantly practiced by the Seventh-day Adventist Church including food distribution, clothing drives, and health education classes. It is, however, those "non-traditional community services such as job finding and job training programs, senior citizen activities, family counseling, and substance abuse programs that correlate with church growth."[83]

In terms of the effectiveness of the worship service and its relationship to evangelism, "worship services designed for the unchurched, including 'seeker services' or special Sabbaths aimed at non-members such as 'Friend Day'" attribute to the growth of the church. Additionally, "one of the most effective evangelistic methods in Adventist churches today is adding a second or additional worship service on Sabbath afternoon or Friday night. Fast growing congregations are nearly twice as likely to have two or more services that are 'very different' in worship style, while in

---

[82]Ibid.

[83]Ibid., 21.

stable and declining congregations it is more likely that the services are similar in style."[84]

Summary

In a recent newspaper article entitled "Church Study Finds Diversity, Lack of Discord Boost Growth," as published in the *Atlanta Journal Constitution*, three primary characteristics were attributed to congregational growth in America. John Blake, writer of this article, said that "thriving congregations tend to be multiracial, embraced vibrant worship services, and avoided major conflict."[85] He also reported that congregations that are most likely to grow include those that attract a larger proportion of men, use drums or percussion during worship, adopt a specific plan to recruit new members, establish a church website, and offer support groups such as marriage counseling, 12-step programs, and wellness programs.[86] Ironically, the characteristics of the growing churches mentioned above closely mirror the social and economic influences that are prevalent in our contemporary society,

---

[84]Ibid., 23.

[85]John Blake, "Church Study Finds Diversity, Lack of Discord Boost Growth," *Atlanta Journal Constitution*, January 29, 2007, C-1.

[86]Ibid.

including the increased expression employed in worship, intentionality on recruitment through relationships and attractive ministries and programs, use of innovative technology, and urban outreach initiatives.

Now whether it is accepted or not, the realities of our religious society exist, and as the old adage goes, "It is what it is." Candidly, "one of the primary reasons that churches stop growing is the way they do, or don't do, evangelism."[87] William G. Johnsson, former editor in chief of *Adventist Review*, official publication of the Seventh-day Adventist Church, comments on the outlook of American Christianity with the statement, "Many developments suggest to me that the church is in ferment. More than 50 million adults go to church every weekend, but religion tends to be superficial. The church as a whole does not have a big impact on society. I sense a dissatisfaction with the established institutions of religion, and a hunger for something that will feed the spirit."[88]

In current American culture, change is inevitable and there has been a paradigm shift in relationship to the needs and expectations of the church in America. Ron Gladden

---

[87]Gladden, 42.

[88]William G. Johnsson, "Four Big Questions," *Adventist Review*, May 25, 2006, 10.

acknowledges this paradigm shift and offers four evangelistic responses to it: [89]

1. The goal of the Gospel Commission is to make disciples.
2. Evangelism is not an event, but a process.
3. Some terms need to be redefined including "evangelism," which encompasses everything a church does, along with the term "evangelist," which means reaping specialist.
4. The Gospel Commission does not say, "Come," it says, "Go."

In synopsis, evangelism and church growth writers insist that people's mindsets, desires, and thinking are drastically different today than they were in preceding years relative to religion and spirituality. These differences are largely due to the social, economic, physical, technological, industrial, and philosophical changes in our society. As a result, prior to an evangelistic strategic plan being conceptualized and then implemented, recognition that these changes are existent must be first acknowledged. Without this recognition, effective evangelism will not be realized.

---

[89]Ibid., 51-59.

Barna encapsulates this recognition with the following two statements, "Whether or not you currently understand the implications of these [societal] trends, two things are true. First, you don't have to like the outcomes of things you cannot change, but you do have to deal with them. Second, the more you can anticipate some of the transitions resulting from these trends, the greater will be your ability to help shape the world in ways that are likely to honor God and advance your spiritual maturity. This will impact your own life and the lives of others with whom you interact."[90]

He further expounds, "New types of organizations will replace the inert stalwarts. Seminaries will be challenged to become relevant or move over. Christian colleges, secondary schools, and elementary schools will be challenged to be more overtly and pragmatically Christian in their endeavors. A more diverse continuum of service entities will blossom as believers seek ways to use their skills, money, and time in an effective and life-changing manner."[91]

---

[90]Barna, 48.

[91]Ibid., 108.

CHAPTER 4

HISTORICAL REVIEW OF TWENTIETH CENTURY SEVENTH-DAY ADVENTIST EVANGELISTIC PRACTICES IN THE UNITED STATES

Evangelism Methods

Evangelism in the United States was practiced in a myriad of ways during the twentieth century, but the primary public methods as employed by the Seventh-day Adventist Church during this period included literature evangelism, branch Sabbath School classes, Vacation Bible Schools, weeks of prayer, revivals, tent evangelism, Revelation (and Prophecy) Seminars, and media evangelism. All of these methods contributed to the numeric growth the collective Seventh-day Adventist Church experienced during this period.

The frequency and popularity of these aforementioned practices, however, changed with the shifting societal trends and the corresponding evolutionary effects it had on American residents. With society's aggressive expansion in technology and multi-media, the coming of age for America's "baby boomers," and the migration to suburban areas to name a few, a greater demand was created for a wider array of evangelistic offerings to most effectively reach the growing diversity as reflected in American society. Therefore, the evangelistic methods had to be properly appropriated to the analogous context, period, milieu, and demographic during the 20th century.

Description of Methods

Literature Evangelism

Literature Evangelism, consisting of "door to door" book sales and the distribution of free literature, was very prevalent during this period. In fact, it was through the printed page that many individuals accepted the Seventh-day Adventist message. Ellen White stated earlier, "There are many places in which the voice of the minister cannot be heard, places which can be reached only by our publications–the books, papers, and tracts filled with the Bible truths that the people need."[92]

The benefits of successful literature evangelism were not, however, limited to direct baptisms through reading. Indirectly, literature evangelism "sowed the field" inclusive of dark counties where the "Adventist light" had not be shone, laying sufficient

---

[92]Ellen G. White, *Colporteur Ministry* (Boise, ID: Pacific Press Publishing Association, 1953), 4.

groundwork for future preaching revivals, tent efforts, and reaping meetings. Subsequent to the sale and free distribution of books and other literature, numerous individuals would become members of the Seventh-day Adventist Church after hearing the word that corresponded to the initial reading of the Word, and accompanying books and materials.

Branch Sabbath School

Branch Sabbath School classes, conducted generally as a branch of an established Sabbath School preferably on Saturdays,[93] were also plenteous during this period. Like literature evangelism, branch Sabbath School classes, where individuals taught the Sabbath School lesson to non Seventh-day Adventists, laid positive foundations for future public evangelism initiatives and were particularly beneficial when attempting to evangelize an area where there was no Adventist presence.

Entering a community with invitations of a Bible class to be held among community residents was widely accepted. As individuals learned from the teachings of the Bible, they often accepted these teachings and desired to have the teachings intensify and continue, resulting in their being baptized.

---

[93]Seventh-day Adventist Encyclopedia, 1990 ed., s.v. "Branch Sabbath School."

Additionally, branch Sabbath School classes were effective means of evangelism as practiced by the laity. During this period, the Seventh-day Adventist Church was highly rural, and a good number of rural churches were a part of multi-church districts pastored by one minister. Often the larger church within the district demanded greater time from the district pastor, which often rendered the smaller church(es) with lessened availability and accessibility from the district pastor. Therefore, branch Sabbath School classes afforded the local church leadership including elders, deacons, and Sabbath School teachers, the opportunity of evangelizing their respective communities. Moreover, many of these lay leaders lacked formal ministerial training from an Adventist educational institution, so fittingly, they were able to instruct non Adventist attendees using the Sabbath School lesson as their Bible Study Guide.

Vacation Bible School

Vacation Bible Schools, very similar to branch Sabbath Schools in the instructive component, were highly effective relative to evangelizing children. Often held during the summer vacation period typically for one or two weeks, the Vacation Bible School was held daily under the supervision of the local Sabbath School department of the church. The program of the Vacation Bible School was "centered on Bible lessons and Bible stories, quizzes, songs, games, arts, and crafts and was conducted for children primarily from four to twelve years of age."[94]

Many children were baptized as a result of the Vacation Bible School Program, along with the child's interest in spiritual matters being the catalyst for their parents becoming interested in the same. Like the preceding forms of evangelism, Vacation Bible School laid adequate groundwork for future evangelistic initiatives including preaching revivals and tent meetings.

Weeks of Prayer and Church Revivals

Weeks of Prayer and church revivals were also frequent during this period. Weeks of Prayer were usually held in the early part of November in harmony with the printing of special issues of the *Adventist Review*, the official publication of the Seventh-day Adventist Church, which offered special sermons and readings by various authors for this designated period.[95] An alternative to the typical reading of the *Adventist Review* articles was the actual preaching by ministers in Week of Prayer services. Some churches also offered a Youth Week of Prayer in the spring of the year, which primarily served as a preaching service.

---

[94]Ibid., s.v. "Vacation Bible School."

[95]Ibid., s.v. "Week of Prayer."

Often a reaping initiative in nature, the Week of Prayer service was held nightly for one week in a worship service format usually consisting of song service, prayer, special music, and preaching or the reading of the Week of Prayer article. This week of spiritual emphasis would culminate on Sabbath mornings in the corporate, collective worship service of the church with the goal of bringing individuals to decision and commitment resulting in baptism.[96]

The typical church revival or evangelistic service, held in the local church, civic or school auditoriums, or public halls, also primarily consisted of a format akin to the Week of Prayer service excluding the specially designated reading from the *Adventist Review*. The church revival usually lasted, but was not limited to, three weeks with the purpose of bringing non Seventh-day Adventists to a decision for baptism, and bringing revival, renewal, and rejuvenation to Seventh-day Adventist members.

Additionally, the Sunday night revival service was very common during this period. While the Sunday night revival service resembled the three week revival or crusade in program format, the Sunday night service provided for a weekly, systematic worship service that was intentional of evangelizing non Seventh-

---

[96]Ibid.

day Adventists and introducing the Seventh-day Adventist message.

Neither the Week of Prayer nor revival services, however, were held in great duration, as Weeks of Prayer lasted for one week and revival services typically lasted for three weeks. Consequently, it was often difficult to introduce all of the fundamental doctrines of the Seventh-day Adventist Church in such a limited time frame. Hence, the Week of Prayer and revival services primarily served as very strong reaping initiatives leading to baptisms. The baptism of individuals at the conclusion of these initiatives consummated the evangelistic process which began from original seeds that had been sown through former literature evangelist campaigns, branch Sabbath Schools, and Vacation Bible School programs.

Tent Evangelism

A very productive public evangelistic method yielding large numbers of baptisms during this period was tent evangelism. From north to south and east to west, countless "tent efforts" were held across the United States in efforts to win individuals to Jesus Christ. Conference leadership, particularly in regional conferences, heavily promoted this method and often sponsored major tent meetings in city-wide campaigns among principal cities within their conference territory.[97]

Tent efforts drew hundreds of attendees each evening in the "open air" environment. Passersby were common, along with persons who had been directly recruited through handbills, flyers, and personal contacts. Individuals were attracted to the "Big Tent," and all the hysteria associated with it including its construction, outdoor sign, and bustling activity.

The nightly tent meeting service was usually held six nights per week for periods of six weeks or greater. The service format included song service, opening prayer, welcome, quiz time, which served as the tracking mechanism for identifying visitors and their accompanying demographic information, offering, special music, and the sermon, whose titles were epitomized by catchy, thought provoking phrases or clichés.[98] Additionally, visual aids in the form of chalkboards and video screens were used in which text and pictures complimenting sermon material were shown on a slide projector.

Catering to the felt needs of the community, the tent meeting service was lively and enthusiastic to say the least, as

---

[97]Pastor William C. Jones, retired Southwest Region Conference President, interview by author, December 4, 2005.

[98]Ibid.

reflected in the music, hospitality, and sermon presentation.[99] Churches would rally behind the preacher of the tent effort, also known as the evangelist who could have been a guest evangelist or local church pastor, assisting with distributing handbills and flyers, giving Bible Studies, offering special music, ushering, and engaging in social service initiatives including medical/dental services, clothing distribution, and food giveaways.[100]

The social service initiatives were very beneficial to the residents of the American inner city during this period. Providing free medical and dental services, clothing, and food to inner city residents where most of these tents were situated satisfied their basic, human needs. Independent of one's decision to be baptized, engaging in this type of ministry was God-ordained, given the biblical mandate to feed the hungry and clothe the naked (Matt 25:34-36).

Furthermore, these social service initiatives positively impacted the publicity for the tent campaign given the positive response among residents who were attracted to and attended the nightly tent services as a result of their basic, human needs being

---

[99]James R. Doggette, "Emotion and Rationality in African American Seventh-day Adventist Worship" (D.Min. dissertation, School of Theology at Claremont, 1992), 85-86, 91.

[100]Earl E. Cleveland, *Let the Church Roll On* (Nampa, ID: Pacific Press Publishing Association, 1997), 52-53.

met. Many individuals who were baptized in these tent efforts were initially attracted to the tent due to the social services that were being offered free of charge, heeding the words of Ellen White as mentioned in Chapter 2 that "the Savior mingled with men as one who desired their good. He showed His sympathy for them, ministered to their needs, and won their confidence. Then He bade them, 'Follow Me.'"[101]

Vacation Bible School programs were often held simultaneously with the tent meetings during the day or just prior to the nightly meetings, and were an effective recruiting tool for children as well as their parents.

Revelation (or Prophecy) Seminar

Another public evangelistic method that was being used in the United States was the prophecy or *Revelation Seminar*. Originally the brainchild of veteran Seventh-day Adventist evangelist, George Knowles, in the early 1970s, seminars were held all day on Sabbaths where individuals were invited to come and study the Bible. When Knowles accepted an invitation to join the *It Is Written* staff, he shared the seminar idea with its director, George Vandeman, stating that given the demand of Vandeman's preaching schedule, Vandeman could conduct one day seminars in

---

[101] White, *Ministry of Healing*, 143.

varying cities as opposed to spending weeks in one city conducting reaping meetings. At this one day seminar, television viewers could initially attend, and then local church pastors would follow up the one day seminar with a series of eighteen evening seminars. "The seminars would be named *Revelation Seminar*, applying the word 'revelation' in the sense that the entire Bible was a revelation of God's message to humanity."[102]

The plan was a success from the start. As demand increased, the series was launched with evening seminars as well as all day seminars. The *Revelation Seminar* Lessons were uniformly supplied by Seminars Unlimited, a resource distribution center for the Seventh-day Adventist Ministerial Association, Continuing Education, and Shepherdess International, and included twenty-four primary lessons for seminar attendees.[103] The *Seventh-day Adventist Encyclopedia* says that "the Revelation Seminars became the most predictable form of evangelism, as it appealed to a sophisticated generation accustomed to business and educational seminars. Pastors who did not have the flair for public evangelism but who did have the gift for teaching discovered that they could win souls through this approach. These developments

---

[102]Seventh-day Adventist Encyclopedia, 1990 ed., s.v. "Revelation Seminar."

[103]Ibid.

came at a time when it was becoming more difficult to attract the public as well as church members to conventional evangelistic meetings."[104]

Media Evangelism

To keep pace with the changing societal trends, and seeking to remain true to the divine mandate of evangelism, numerous radio and television ministries were utilized during this period. National and local media ministries including, but not limited to, *Breath of Life, Faith for Today, It Is Written, Voice of Prophecy, La Voz de la Esperanza, Lifestyle Magazine, The Quiet Hour, Adventist World Radio, Life Talk Radio, Three Angels' Broadcasting Network (3ABN), Hope Channel, and Loma Linda Broadcasting Network* were all media evangelism tools successfully employed during the 20th century, which led countless individuals to baptism into the Seventh-day Adventist Church.

Additionally, the genesis of the internet spurned many Adventist web streaming ministries, affording individuals across the country to view worship services via the internet, along with the birth of the "Net" evangelistic series. The "Net" evangelistic series was an innovative form of satellite evangelism, where utilizing modern technology and the internet, individuals at

---

[104]General Conference of Seventh-day Adventists, Office of Statistics.

numerous downlink sites across the globe could witness the preaching ministry of evangelists in another location. Subsequently, individuals would be baptized and join local Seventh-day Adventist congregations.

Societal Changes

It is obvious that the historical evangelistic methods described thus far had previously served as effective tools in reaching individuals earlier in the twentieth century given the total membership growth of the Seventh-day Adventist Church in the United States. Yet, their relevance and effectiveness in reaching the masses in the twenty-first century appears to be waning given the infrequency of their use and the declining total annual and per capita baptisms.[105]

What are the reasons for this decline? Postmodernism and urban growth, as cited in Chapter 3, have already been identified as having a rising impact on societal religious trends and norms in the United States. While they are key emerging influences promoting the need for contemporary evangelism, there are two additional reasons worth mentioning that have had an "evolutionary" effect on both the decline in the number of total and per capita baptisms

---

[105]Ibid.

in the United States, and the diminished employment of historical evangelistic methods as practiced in the twentieth century. They are: increased secularization and growing affluence.

Increased Secularization

Increased secularization can be rooted in the words of 1 John 2:15, 16, "If any man love the world, the love of the Father (God) is not in him. For all that is in the world, the lust of the flesh, and the lust of the eyes, and the pride of life, is not of the Father, but is of the world." This text underscores the reality that given our increasingly secularized society, it is becoming increasingly difficult socially, economically, physically, and spiritually for individuals to become desirous of adapting to the Seventh-day Adventist message and the lifestyle it promotes.

Current American culture, reminiscent of the biblical days of Noah and the cultures of Sodom and Gomorrah respectively (Matt 24:37, 38; Gen 18, 19), is highly secular. As a result of this soaring secularization, its impact has desensitized the importance of religious conviction and reduced the value of morality, producing a climate that says, "If it feels good, do it." C. Eric Lincoln and Lawrence H. Mamiya in their work, *The Black Church in the African American Experience*, support this viewpoint as it relates to the black church in America, which I believe, transcends to all ethnic cultures within America. They state, "The process of secularization in (black) communities has always meant a diminishing of the influence of religion and an erosion in the central importance of (black) churches. Secularization is accompanied by the twin processes of increasing differentiation and increasing pluralism that tend to diminish the cultural unity provided by the (black) sacred cosmos, (the church)."[106]

Growing Affluence

Another explanation for this per capita decline in baptisms is the aspiration of collective society to increase in wealth and riches. 1 Timothy 6:10 says, "For the love of money is the root of all evil." Consequently, this passion, zeal, and desire for money, coupled with the accessibility of the educational and vocational opportunities for life enrichment has fostered a growing affluence among all Americans. This growing affluence has further produced an expanding physical and social isolation between economic classes in the United States, prompting many individuals to physically shift from the urban to the suburban areas of America's metropolitan areas. Therefore, the Seventh-day Adventist Church's physical impact and influence has been lost to the geographically distant group producing weakened attendance at

---

[106]C. Eric Lincoln and Lawrence H. Mamiya, *The Black Church in the African American Experience* (Durham, NC: Duke University Press, 1990), 383.

weekly services, programs, evangelistic initiatives, and ministerial endeavors.

As one flourishes in "milk and honey," the conscious and unconscious need for dependence on the supernatural or a "higher power" commonly bears the propensity to diminish. Reliance on God and commitment to the church often weaken as one increases in wealth and opulence. Rev 3:17 magnifies this concept, "Because thou sayest, I am rich, and increased with goods, and have need of nothing; and knowest not that thou art wretched, and miserable, and poor, and blind, and naked."

Julia Duin, in an article written in *The Washington Times*, states that "although the number of committed Christians (both black and white) grew from 35 percent of the faithful in 1995 to 41 percent in 2000, weekly church attendance, however, dropped from the 49 percent to 43 percent. Further, the numbers enrolling in Bible study and adult Sunday School or volunteering for religious activities have shrunk."[107]

The budding prosperity among Americans has afforded many individuals not only the educational benefits of such affluence, but also amplified social exposure and experiences. Accordingly, the high technological age we live in as evidenced by

---

[107] Julia Duin, "New Breed Preachers Defy Traditions," *The Washington Times*, July 6, 2001.

computer advances, the internet, the world wide web, audio-visual improvements, and electronic enhancements, joined with increased exposure of the populace in general, has elevated expectations regarding the modalities and methodologies of how we do "church" as a people. As a result, the Seventh-day Adventist Church must evaluate its effectiveness in the proclamation of the gospel. More specifically, the seasonal evangelistic campaign may have been successful in former years, but its effectiveness appears to be antiquated in our postmodern era and may have reached its expiration period given society's "instant gratification ethic."

The Call for New Evangelistic Methods

The challenges of high secularization and the socioeconomic increases of Americans in general, along with rising postmodernism and urban growth demand that the Seventh-day Adventist Church must change and alter its evangelistic methodologies that are structured for older generations to meet this paradigm shift. Change is inevitable as we usher in the twenty-first century. Societal thoughts, actions, behaviors, and desires have changed, and societal attitudes toward Christendom and its presentation are not immune to this shift.

The effectiveness and relevancy of traditional methods of evangelism that were formerly used by Seventh-day Adventists in previous periods have diminished given these changes. Based on the reasons previously mentioned, their corresponding applications are as follows. Security concerns, changing demographics, and environmental discomfort weaken the effectiveness of tent evangelism. Increased education and employment limit church participation in daily evangelistic initiatives including Vacation Bible School, church revivals, and Weeks of Prayer. The creation of the internet, and the overall growth of information technology, affect the marketing of products in new ways with new products and new processes,[108] which consequently negatively impact "door to door" literature evangelism sales and Bible study solicitation.

To fulfill its stated mission, the Seventh-day Adventist Church will need to adopt new and progressive evangelistic methods by engaging in contemporary evangelism in order to reach our diverse, changing, and postmodern society. Ellen White advocated this concept of relevance by stating, "Everyone connected with the work should keep fresh ideas and by tact and foresight bring all that is possible into your work to interest your hearers."[109] She added, "We must work in different ways and

---

[108] Perreault and McCarthy, 86-87.

[109] White, *Evangelism*, 178.

devise different methods, and let God work in us to the revealing of truth and Himself as the sin-pardoning Savior."[110]

To further compound matters, the Seventh-day Adventist Church must face the challenge of developing new evangelistic methodologies in the wake of our evolving, growing metropolitan areas where most American residents are situated. Thorough analysis of Ellen White's writings, in harmony with the Bible as illustrated through the life of Christ, suggests that the church is to go and minister where the people are, which based upon the demographic information as mentioned in Chapter 3 intimate greater emphasis in our cities.

Mrs. White further synthesized her views on the need for city evangelism and the increased difficulty associated with it. She shares this while calling for new evangelistic methods. She says, "We do not realize the extent to which Satanic agencies are at work in these large cities. The work of bringing the message of present truth before the people is becoming more and more difficult. It is essential that new and varied talents unite in intelligent labor."[111]

---

[110]Ibid., 291.

[111]Ellen G. White, *Medical Ministry* (Mountain View, CA: Pacific Press Publishing Association, 1963), 300.

It is logical then to assert that if Ellen White was giving this counsel in 1909,[112] its relevance and application is even more paramount for the present day. New methods, ideas, and strategies are desperately needed for our changing society. Ellen White gave these words of caution at a time when Adventism was just placing root in the United States, let alone the world. In her day, neither the mediums of communication were as widespread as they are today, nor was the globalization of our world as pronounced and prevalent in society in the nineteenth century as it currently is in the twenty-first century given our industrial and technological advances through the use of automobiles, airplanes, television, radio, computers, the internet, etc. Hence, the ability to proclaim the gospel in Ellen White's day was limited due to society's limited communication vehicles. Consequently, on one end of the spectrum, we have witnessed inflation and increased disenfranchisement in our communities today, and contrastingly, we have realized increased economics and education among Americans. Yet, all of these factors have contributed to lessened baptism numbers and weakened evangelistic effectiveness.

If Ellen White's call to modernize our methods and go into our cities with our distinct message was imminent in her era, underscoring the biblical mandate to evangelize, one can only

---

[112]Ibid.

presume that the intensity and necessity of this call is even greater today. We must then reach individuals with evangelistic methods and ministries that appeal to our postmodern context. This does not suggest that we are to compromise biblical doctrine or the Seventh-day Adventist message, but this does advocate the necessity of change and to become sensitive to the needs and wants of the society in which we live. Therefore, the ministerial modalities and accompanying administrative practices of the Seventh-day Adventist Church should harmonize with this shifting population. "He who seeks to transform humanity must himself understand humanity."[113] Church leaders must combine revelation with relevance. "If the church has relevance without revelation, its message will be contemporary but empty of truth. If the church has revelation without relevance, its message will be true, but it will not be understood or accepted."[114]

---

[113] White, *Education*, 78.

[114] Calvin B. Rock, "Black Seventh-day Adventist Preaching: Balanced and Binding or Betwixt and Between?" *Black Seventh-day Adventist Preaching: Its Relevance for the New Millennium*, April 19-20, 2000, 20-27.

CHAPTER 5

DESIGN OF THE CONTEMPORARY EVANGELISM PLAN

Theoretical Cognizance

It is imperative that theoretical principles be identified and embraced prior to their practical application in order to generate optimum success. Therefore, in order for "buy in" to transpire relative to the adoption of contemporary evangelistic methodologies, there must first be an acknowledgement on the part of the local church as to why the church must grow, including full recognition that the primary purpose of the church is the evangelization of the world (Matt 28:19, 20).

The church should recognize where it is in effectively promulgating the gospel of Jesus Christ with specificity to its geographic location, and identify where it needs to go before practically attempting to get there. This recognition can be achieved through a sundry of ways, including pastoral meetings with church leaders, namely the elders and church board, along with meeting with the entire church membership. Additionally, surveys are excellent evaluative instruments that allow members to objectively assess the present state of the church in terms of evangelism. Moreover, through surveys, church leaders and members alike are able to view documented, unbiased responses from all respondents on evangelism, which further promotes "buy-in."

Both the pastor and the church should embrace this need to evangelize, and be willing to pay its accompanying price,[115] including the inevitability of "change" and the adoption of new evangelistic methods[116] given decreased baptism numbers and their relationship to current and future urban, postmodern societal norms. As Paul Harvey once said, "We have been called to be fishers of men, not keepers of the aquarium."[117] Therefore, when developing unconventional evangelistic methodologies, pastors and members alike need to understand that the ultimate reason the church should engage in this process is explicitly tied to the mission of the church and the need to most effectively fulfill it in the era in which we live.

After the church has theoretically identified its current evangelistic position, the pastor should then challenge the church to proceed with a newly identified plan of action. If the pastor

---

[115]Wagner, *Your Church Can Be Healthy*, 24-28.

[116]Finley, 5.

[117]Paul Harvey in Doug Batchelor, "Gone Fishing," *Ministry*, June, 2001, 10.

moves forward without this "buy in," or engaging in this educational process, it could be detrimental to the entire church growth program. Various techniques of this conjectural process include additional surveys, strategic planning sessions, seminars, workshops, departmental meetings, classes, sermon presentations, and "best practices" exercises, including visitation to model churches. The main goal is to get the church to acknowledge the collective church growth challenge in the United States, and to accept the call to contemporary evangelistic methods.

Ron Gladden in his book, *The Seven Habits of Highly Ineffective Churches*, identifies four core ministries of evangelistically effective churches: worship, outreach, discipleship, and administration.[118] While each of these core ministries is pivotal to the growth of a church, it is my belief that worship, outreach, and administration directly impact evangelistic growth, while discipleship is better applicable to a process of retention. Hence, the former three core ministries, in my opinion, serve as springboards to launch an effective contemporary evangelistic plan at a local church and are crucial to the success of this plan. Furthermore, this innovative plan cannot be limited by season or event, but contemporary evangelism calls for the creation

---

[118]Gladden, 116.

of a new evangelistic culture within the church, which is reflected in worship, outreach, and administration.

Worship

Given the societal influences mentioned in Chapter 4 (postmodernism, urban growth, increased secularization, and growing affluence) and their corresponding manifestations, including mindset differences along with the availability and accessibility of individuals, which are negatively impacting traditional evangelistic practices, the importance of worship in the local Seventh-day Adventist Church as a primary tool for evangelism cannot be underscored enough. Monte Sahlin says that "the most effective way to do public evangelism is through the worship service on Sabbath."[119] Kennon L. Callahan in his book, *Twelve Keys to an Effective Church*, adds that "it is highly likely that many of the un-churched persons whom a church reaches in mission or visitation will find their way first to the service of worship."[120] Furthermore, if worship is to contribute to the growth

---

[119]Sahlin, "What Makes Churches Grow? What Recent Adventist Research Reveals," *Ministry*, November , 2004, 6.

[120]Kennon L. Callahan, *Twelve Keys to an Effective Church* (San Francisco, CA: Jossey-Bass Publishers, 1983), 24.

of a church in our current society, three things must be true: members can't wait to attend, members are proud to bring their friends, and whoever attends is eager to return.[121]

Although there are numerous forms of relevant advertising for churches, including television, radio, newspapers, flyers, etc., the greatest form of advertisement for a church is still in its people. When members are excited about the worship experience of their local church, they will want to be present and readily invite others to join them. On the contrary, if they don't want to be present, why would they want anyone else to be present? The old adage is still true, "people breed people," "people win people," and "people want to go where the people are." Strong, growing evangelistic churches exemplify these characteristics as evidenced through the energy and morale of its members. Because of these reasons, worship, I believe, is where the evangelistic renaissance should initially begin.

Synthesis of Myron Augsburger's definition of evangelism and C. Raymond Holmes' definition of worship accentuate the need for vitality in the corporate worship setting to foster evangelistic growth. In his book, *Invitation to Discipleship*,

---

[121]Gladden, 81-83.

Augsburger expresses that "evangelism is the life of the church;[122] and Holmes states that, "the life, the heartbeat of the church is worship."[123] Holmes also adds that "evangelism is the consequence, the natural and powerful outgrowth or result, of the church's worship life. It is corporate worship that is truly missionary and evangelistic in nature."[124] Therefore, evangelism is stimulated and fueled by corporate, dynamic worship – one of the twelve keys, as cited by Callahan.[125]

In Matt 11:28, Jesus said, "Come unto Me," and then He said in Matt 28:19-20, "Go ye into all the world." Holmes in his aforementioned book calls to our attention that the word "come" precedes "go." God is calling us to come to Him in worship and praise and then go out into the world. Holmes believes that the Seventh-day Adventist Church in worship should be evangelistic in nature, form, and function.[126] He continues:

---

[122]Myron Augsburger, *Invitation to Discipleship* (Scottdale, PA: Herald Press, 1967), 1.

[123]C. Raymond Holmes, *Sing a New Song* (Berrien Springs, MI: Andrews University Press, 1984), 136.

[124]Ibid., 136-37.

[125]Callahan, 24-33.

[126]Holmes, 137.

The church was not created solely for God, however, it was also created for the world. It is only when the church understands and appreciates its call to worship that it can understand and appreciate its call to evangelize. When the church gathers for worship, the world is there too. In the gathering of the church, it becomes apparent to the world that the people of God are to live. The corporate body of Christ, by means of its individual members, must permeate society and culture in righteous and holy living. This is living evangelistically. In that sense the gathered church is scattered into the world.[127]

If worship is to reflect evangelism and serve as a primary vehicle to facilitate the winning of individuals to Jesus Christ, then the vivacious expressions of energy and enthusiasm as used in the typical evangelistic service should be employed in the corporate worship service fostering evangelistic growth while simultaneously promoting positive morale. Moreover, a worship service that emulated such energy would neither conflict with the Bible (Psa 100 and 150), nor with the writings of Ellen White.

In fact, Ellen White vehemently supported a worship service that was lively, enthusiastic, and fervent. She did not

---

[127]Ibid., 138.

condone a dead, dry worship service. She verbalized her feelings by stating:

> Our meetings should be made intensely interesting. They should be pervaded with the very atmosphere of heaven. Let there be no long, dry speeches and formal prayers merely for the sake of occupying the time. All should be ready to act their part with promptness, and when their duty is done, the meeting should be closed. Thus the interest will be kept up to the last. This is offering God acceptable worship. His service should be made interesting and attractive and not be allowed to degenerate in a dry dorm. We must live for Christ minute by minute, hour by hour, and day by day; then Christ will dwell in us, and when we meet together, His love will be in our hearts, welling up like a spring in a desert, refreshing all, and making those who are ready to perish, eager to drink of the waters of life.[128]

Christ cannot be proclaimed in a dead, boring fashion. When we consider the life of Christ inclusive of His mission and ministry, Christ's followers cannot help but be excited. "It is the

---

[128] Ellen G. White, *Testimonies for the Church* (Mountain View, CA: Pacific Press Publishing Association, 1948); 9:233.

work of Christ that we celebrate in worship."[129] Moreover, when Christ is celebrated with excitement, energy, and enthusiasm, these emotive feelings are contagious and transmittable to others, which is the Seventh-day Adventist definition of evangelism, "proclaiming the good news of the gospel."[130] Unfortunately, "the worship experience is all too often a reason why churches stop growing. The pastor can organize plenty of ministry teams, the facility can be attractive and have plenty of space for expansion, relationships can be healthy, and the church members can all be evangelists, but if the worship is dead, the church will not reach the lost."[131]

When one considers the growth of the evangelistic churches in the United States at present, one must conclude that their corporate worship services are dynamic to say the least and possess the vivacious elements mentioned above. These churches represent a new brand of growing churches that are highly participatory, fellowship driven, and embrace enthusiastic worship experiences. "Mainline churches are too bureaucratic. Their message is ambiguous, lacking authority, and their worship is

---

[129] Richard E. Webber, *Worship Is a Verb* (Nashville, TN: Abott-Martyn, 1992), 16.

[130] *Seventh-day Adventist Church Manual*, 90.

[131] Gladden, 80.

anemic."[132] Careful observation of these churches that espouse vibrant worship modalities will enable one to witness the magnetic attraction of these burgeoning congregations.

This should come as no surprise for when Seventh-day Adventist Churches engaged in corporate evangelistic meetings in the twentieth century. Whether it was the tent revival, auditorium revival, or hall meeting, an evangelistic tenor was imitated and manifested, attracting large numbers of visitors to the meetings. Many of these visitors began studying the doctrines of the Seventh-day Adventist Church as presented at these meetings, and subsequently became baptized members of the Seventh-day Adventist Church, only to feel later that perhaps what they had joined, a strong Bible based, enthusiastic fellowship, had been later abandoned upon the end of the evangelistic campaign for a more subdued modality. Nevertheless, because many Seventh-day Adventists now view some of these same twentieth century methods as practices of the past, the frequency and support of their employment have decreased greatly.

Yet, in harmony with the biblical principle that "there's nothing new under the sun" (Eccl 1:9), many characteristics of

---

[132]Duin, "Resuscitating Spiritual Passion," *The Washington Times*, July 6, 2001, A-1.

these meetings should be employed in corporate worship to promote evangelism and church growth. The first characteristic adopted would be a "revival" worship service, inclusive of intentional hospitality, audio-visual enhancements, lively music reflecting simple, praise choruses and hymns, and passionate, inspiring, and Bible-based preaching identified by captivating titles. I surmise that if these elements were incorporated in the corporate worship services of our local churches, it would help create an evangelistic culture conducive to baptismal growth in conformity with Acts 17:16-34. Hence, we would not be engaging so much in a new model, but rather an old model, re-emerging from its former place in biblical and Seventh-day Adventist history, making it applicable to present, contemporary culture.

Put another way, if vivacious music, energetic preaching, and participatory fellowship were successful in attracting individuals to the "revival" service, then why abandon these successful evangelistic elements in the corporate worship service? Carlyle Stewart, III, expresses:

> Vitality is contagious. If people can show excitement for the cars they drive, the homes they live in, the teams they support, why can't Christians show joy for Jesus? If anything kills a viable evangelism program, it is the lack of ardor by those called to witness to God's love and truth as revealed in their lives.

Joy should be made manifest in everything, from personal witnessing to the experience of worship. People, as a rule, don't tell people about a dead church. They won't invite people to a church if it lacks the spiritual propellants that drive and uplift the human spirit, that dispel depression, doubt, and despondency. People want a church that's alive and stimulating. They want to be with people who share the joy of living life through Christ.[133]

Moreover, "baby boomers, baby busters, and the unchurched are (primarily) interested in a participative, high-energy worship experience. The low-energy, passive presentation-style worship service (primarily) appeals to the older generation, but fails to reach those raised in the television and internet era."[134] While we have different constituencies in which we service, "our greatest constituency should be the millions, who, unless something changes between now and Jesus' coming, will not be

---

[133]Carlyle F. Stewart, III, *African American Church Growth: Twelve Principles for Ministry* (Nashville, TN: Abingdon Press, 1994), 131.

[134]Lyle Schaller, *What Have We Learned* (Nashville, TN: Abingdon Press, 2002), 23.

going to heaven."[135] Jesus said, "I came not to call the righteous, but sinners to repentance" (Matt 9:13).

Outreach

The second core ministry area that would help foster this contemporary evangelistic culture is outreach. While outreach can have diverse meanings, our discussion will be limited to three primary areas as it relates to contemporary evangelism. They are: 1) community outreach, 2) community visitation, and 3) the public evangelistic campaign.

Community Outreach

Successful contemporary evangelism comprises meeting people's felt needs and expressing love towards them in a relevant way. This means taking the ministry of the church beyond the four walls of the church, and genuinely addressing the needs of the church's community. The local church pastor is not solely called to pastor the church, but rather called to pastor the community. The barometer to gauge the effectiveness of a church's outreach ministry is measured by the following question, "If our church

---

[135]Ron Gladden, "Building a Home Depot," (*Mission Catalyst Network*: n.p., 2001), 12.

were to leave this community, would we be missed by our neighboring residents?"

Neighborhood residents need to see that the church is not merely interested in gaining more members and money, but that it is most interested in the well-being and positive development of people. "People seek out churches who give themselves away. People stay away from those churches whose only interest is self-interest. When people have specific hurts and hopes, they are amazed and surprised to discover a congregation that is genuinely interested in being of help to them."[136]

Historically, the Seventh-day Adventist Church made a significant impact in the lives of community residents during the twentieth century. Some examples of this included local community service ministries, which provided numerous traditional community initiatives including food, clothing, and furniture distribution, along with health programs which offered cooking classes, medical screening, counseling, and referrals to community residents. Nevertheless, as our United States' population has increased and diversified, coupled with the symptoms of the times in which we live, community social ills have also increased and/or intensified. As a result of this amplification, our outreach initiatives must better address these

---

[136]Callahan, 9.

challenges by offering more relevant, appropriate community ministry to our postmodern context in hopes of meeting people's felt needs. Although this does not mean total abandonment from the initiatives we have traditionally done well with, it does mean enrichment of our community service offerings to address prominent societal ills including the AIDS epidemic, unemployment, inflation, and teen pregnancy (to name a few).

When referencing the need for relevant community outreach initiatives, Monte Sahlin says:

There has been something of a paradigm shift over the last two decades. Community involvement and visibility have become key issues for church growth. The growing churches are those with significant, non-traditional community services and active relationships with the neighborhood. The community service involvements that correlate with church growth are not the usual activities that we (pastors) often think of as community services. Emergency food distribution, 'Dorcas' clothing programs, and health education classes were not among the items in the cluster. Non-traditional community services such as job-finding and job-training programs, weekly or daily hot meals for neighborhood senior citizens, homeless shelters, family counseling services, and substance-abuse programs are the kinds of things that correlate with church growth.

Church growth correlates with doing a good job of communicating with the community as well as actually providing certain kinds of services. Thus, church growth is more likely to occur when a congregation has a visible role in the community and when its service activities are seen as community-based rather than the traditional church-based community service paradigm."[137]

While the needs of the community are limitless, an effective church has one or two major outreach ministries that it is known for in the community.[138] Therefore, rather than being a "jack of all trades" and "master of none," it is necessary to pursue attainable and relevant outreach goals that could be realized and performed in an outstanding manner – particularly given a church's resources.

Hence, a church's primary niche could be a food distribution program, drug counseling, GED classes, AIDS awareness, and the list could continue. Nevertheless, engagement in some form of outreach is necessary for many reasons, but I would like to cite three. Number one, outreach provides needed help for community residents. Within the cities of our nation,

---

[137]Sahlin, 6.

[138]Callahan, 3.

where the majority of individuals reside, the social, physical, educational, and economic needs are abundant. Noted evangelist, Alejandro Bullon, says:

> Deep inside them is a great emptiness from which they cannot free themselves. They can deny it, they can pretend that they do not feel it, they can disguise it, but loneliness consumes them day and night. Friendships derived in social clubs, parties, and public places are empty and superficial. People need to feel accepted and loved as individuals, and not just used. They need to know that someone is interested in their struggles and conflicts. Christians should understand these emotional essentials and authentically come close to these lonely individuals and present them to the Lord Jesus Christ and the fellowship of His family.[139]

Second, outreach promotes spiritual and social growth for church members. We can never stop growing, and it is God's will for us to continue to grow in our Christian walk (Phil 1:6). "Mission leads us beyond ourselves. Whenever a local congregation is effectively engaged in missionary outreach, that congregation is a group of people living beyond their preoccupation with

---

[139] Alejandro Bullon, "Reaching the Cities," *Ministry*, June, 2001, 12.

themselves."[140] Put simply, we help ourselves when we help others.

Third, outreach enables us to build relationships and create public awareness of the overall ministry of the church, which is crucial to the image of the Seventh-day Adventist Church. Clearly a minority denomination in American Christianity with only a little over one million members in a nation of over 300 million,[141] and perceived by many as different, even cultic in some circles,[142] Seventh-day Adventists must positively impact the community in significant ways to help combat this perception of being socially irrelevant to the societal challenges of the present day.

Community Visitation

Another means of contemporary evangelistic outreach is strong community visitation. Community visitation should not be confused with community visibility. While community visibility, including the use of media - television, radio, print, and the internet, along with the previously mentioned community outreach

---

[140]General Conference of Seventh-day Adventists, Office of Statistics; United States Census Bureau.

[141]Callahan, 3.

[142]Josh McDowell and Don Stewart, *Handbook of Today's Religions* (Nashville, TN: Thomas Nelson Publishers, 1983), 558.

initiatives, focuses on mass communication to community residents, community visitation concentrates on direct interaction and individual involvement with community residents.

One of the greatest ways to engage in this community visitation is realized through the employment of staff members or Bible Instructors who visit community residents on a systematic basis. Traditionally, this philosophy is advocated during seasonal public evangelism campaigns, but in our contemporary, postmodern world of high technology and growing affluence, individuals engaged in remunerated church ministry are truly needed in our churches to facilitate consistent visitation on a daily basis particularly within our inner-city communities. We clearly can no longer expect people to come to us, but we must go to them. Ellen White stresses the importance of "door to door" visitation by stating, "Not only is the truth to be presented in public assemblies; house-to-house work is to be done. Let this work go forward in the name of the Lord. This house-to-house labor, searching for souls, hunting for the lost sheep, is the most essential work that can be done."[143]

The call for increased community presence, along with the decreased availability, accessibility, and accountability of church members, dictate that the traditional Seventh-day Adventist Pastor

---

[143] White, *Evangelism*, 431.

cannot alone provide the needed, mass community visitation. Additionally, many of our church members no longer reside within the communities where our churches are situated and/or the church structure has relocated to suburban areas from our inner cities, affording "little contact with the community surrounding the local church structure."[144] Therefore, capable, obligatory staff members are needed for the coordinated, assiduous operation of evangelizing souls throughout the calendar year. One might express, "We can't afford to hire Bible Instructors." My response, "You can't afford not to." If the chief responsibility of the church is evangelism in all its phases,[145] then church funding should resonate with this priority.

Although this should not displace membership involvement in the visitation process, it is a proven fact that the infrastructure of the seasonal public evangelistic campaign inclusive of full time Bible Instructors was very productive in evangelizing the masses, particularly those external to the membership of the church. In fact, most, public evangelistic campaigns were not conducted without the use of a Bible Instructor. Hence, if it was prudent to employ individuals during times of intentional, seasonal

---

[144]Sahlin, *What Makes Churches Grow? What Recent Adventist Research Reveals*, 6.

[145]*Seventh-day Adventist Church Manual*, 90.

evangelism, why not adopt a similar arrangement throughout the calendar year? Moreover, membership involvement in visitation would hopefully elevate as members witness others engaging in this activity motivating their desire to join in this evangelistic initiative producing a synergistic effect.

Addressing the importance of community visitation characterized by human interaction, Bullon shares, "In large cities throughout the world, where I have had the opportunity to preach, we have seen, tested, and confirmed that the best means to reach people today is through other human beings."[146] I am in full agreement with Bullon, and believe the importance and value of human interaction through remunerated staff members to accomplish this purpose cannot be stressed enough. Accountable, competent Bible Instructors or staff members are needed to visit community residents, identify and address their human felt needs, counsel with them, and share the love of Jesus with them through Bible study and prayer.

Public Evangelistic Campaign

Although a church should engage in consistent evangelistic activities throughout the calendar year, this should not nullify the

---

[146]Bullon, 12.

seasonal public evangelistic campaign. "It is wrong for a local church to conclude that if they stop doing conventional public evangelism, Revelation Seminars, Bible studies, etc., that they will begin to grow. In fact, these tried-and-true methods work to enhance the process in most growing congregations, although they cannot be expected to grow by themselves."[147]

The public evangelistic meeting should encompass dynamic worship, community outreach, and community visibility. Stressing seeker sensitivity, the public evangelistic campaign should theoretically support the philosophy of historic Adventist evangelism while practically applying the stylistic modalities of current culture including enthusiastic worship, informality, high emphasis on people, employment of technology, and creative doctrinal presentation.

Public evangelistic campaigns are beneficial for both members and visitors alike. For members, they are consistently involved in service, further indoctrinated in the Advent message, and the primacy of evangelism is kept before them. For visitors, they feel a sense of community and fellowship, learn precious Biblical truths, provide an infusion of energy and excitement for the collective church, and many accept Jesus Christ as their personal Savior.

---

[147]Sahlin, 11.

Administration

Given our society's postmodernist emphasis on decentralization, informality, and egalitarianism, administrative levels of the local church should exist to promote greater evangelistic effectiveness and efficiency. Put simply, structure must support mission. The applicable contemporary approach for this practice rests in streamlining or eliminating the "bureaucratic bottleneck" that often plagues the growth of churches through redundant, irrelevant committees and boards, and their accompanying processes.

Streamlined structure and solid, participatory decision making are necessary essentials for an effective church.[148] Politics and emphasis on anything other than the spiritual nurture and welfare of people will steer the membership from the overall mission of the church. "Congregations that have a cumbersome decision-making process will be likely to have a complex organizational structure. By the same token, their complex organizational structure will contribute directly to the cumbersomeness of the decision-making process."[149] Hence, it is

---

[148]Callahan, 55-63.

[149]Ibid., 55.

necessary to streamline bureaucratic church structure and place increased structural emphasis on people to foster church growth.

Vision for the local church should be set by the local pastor.[150] Mindful that two visions are "di-vision," and "vision is not the result of consensus, but should result in consensus,"[151] the church board and membership should assist in the realization of vision, but vision for the local church should originate from the leader. Additionally, church leadership should have the ability to execute the operational affairs of the church while greater concentration on strategies is the responsibility of the church board. Hence, implementation of an appropriate, simple, and accountable structure in which members of the board become supporters of the church leadership that execute everyday decisions is fittingly appropriate.

Such a structure could encompass a new system for committees in the church, reflecting church board composition that calls for four primary committees: worship, ministry, outreach, and administration. These committees should develop ministry plans, that when combined, offer comprehensive, holistic strategies for the church to adopt enabling the evangelistic mission of the church

---

[150]George Barna, *The Power of Vision* (Ventura, CA: Regal Books, 1992), 24, 32.

[151]Ibid., 45.

to be pursued. Furthermore, election and/or appointment of these committees and persons comprising them should be primarily "gifts-based," rather than more heavily weighted towards popularity or membership longevity. It was this "gifts-based" model that was commonly adopted by Seventh-day Adventist churches during seasonal evangelistic campaigns when selecting ushers, greeters, parking attendants, quiz announcers, musicians, etc. If such a model proved successful during that season, and the major goal of the local church is evangelism, then implementation of this model would prove most profitable throughout the calendar year.

CHAPTER 6

APPLICATION OF THE CONTEMPORARY EVANGELISM PLAN

The implementation, or application of contemporary evangelism plans, is vital to the success of the growth of the church. It's one thing to theoretically understand contemporary evangelism principles, but it's another thing to apply them. Hence, this chapter is very practical in nature and devoted to offering suggested methods to apply contemporary evangelism plans.

When a church is desirous of evangelistic growth, a culture of evangelism, as stated in Chapter 5, must be created, which is manifested throughout the life of the church. Everything that is planned, practiced, and "prayed for" should be rooted in evangelism. In harmony with the core ministries shared in Chapter 5, this chapter specifically focuses on the application of worship and outreach methods to create an evangelistic culture in the local church.

Worship

In order to properly create an evangelistic culture in worship, I would like to propose that worship cannot be merely limited to a "service," but rather worship must be an "experience." Webster defines service as, "acts of devotion to God; witness; religious rite," whereas experience is defined as "active participation in events or activities, leading to the accumulation of knowledge or skill; an event or series of event participated in or lived through."[152] Worship should consist of more than just an event or service, but a series of events or activities that lead attendees into the expression of their love and devotion to God. This series of events, or experience, inclusive of all the elements of worship given their importance to effective evangelism, begins upon an individual's arrival at the church and ends at this same person's departure. Given this, the worship experience includes three areas: warmth and hospitality of the congregation, worship service, and worship leadership.

Warmth and Hospitality of the Congregation

Because the worship experience begins at the arrival of a church attendee (as appropriate to this book), the warmth and hospitality of the congregation should be evident upon the visitor's arrival to the church. The manner in which an individual is received as he/she arrives at the church sets the tone for the entire

---

[152]Webster's Dictionary (1990), s.v. "Worship."

worship experience of the individual. To better ensure this warm reception, there should be intentional and careful selection of persons who minister in service ministries, namely parking supervisors, ushers, greeters, and worship leaders.

All too often in the Seventh-day Adventist Church, emphasis and priority is placed on the selection of administrative personnel (Elders, Deacons, Deaconesses, Clerks, Treasurers, etc.) and departmental ministry personnel (Sabbath School, Personal Ministries, Adventist Youth Society, etc.), while the equivalent primacy is not mirrored in the selection of service ministry personnel. Nominating committees will deliberate and mull over administrative and departmental ministry positions and often place their selection at the beginning of the election process, and consequently, when it is time to select service ministry personnel, individuals are often selected on availability as opposed to ability and spiritual giftedness as many nominating committees want the grueling process of church election to end and many of these service ministry positions are not church board related positions. Nevertheless, if the worship experience is to be one that promotes evangelism and church growth, the same emphasis that is placed on administrative and departmental personnel should be given to the selection of service ministry personnel.

This primacy of service ministry personnel is not foreign to the church – for as in seasonal evangelistic campaigns, it has long been practiced that specific individuals in harmony with their spiritual giftedness would serve as parking attendants, ushers, greeters, and worship leaders in public evangelistic campaigns, not to mention the training that took place prior to evangelistic activities. If this was practiced for the evangelistic campaign, why wouldn't it be practiced at the church on an annual basis?

Churches should engage in the intentional selection of these service ministry personnel who condone and endorse the concept of an enthusiastic evangelistic culture at the church, coupled with providing training that emphasizes "seeker-sensitivity" and customer service with the goal of producing a positive climate that is conducive to the receptivity of the word of God. Proper and genuine greeting, sensitivity to parking and seat selection, inclusive accommodation in word and action, friendliness, and a general love for people should epitomize these service individuals.

The other officers of the church are not exempt from assisting in the evangelistic culture of the church. The environment of "seeker-sensitivity" and inclusion in the worship experience should be fostered by all church officers (administrative, departmental, and service). The importance of making each attendee, church member and/or visitor feel special is the duty of every church officer. Every individual who enters the church doors is to be accepted and viewed as a candidate for church membership, while every church member should be appreciated and respected with the goal of one hundred percent retention. Moreover, it is the responsibility of every church officer to be a soul winner and exemplify this goal through his/her respective ministry in the corporate worship experience and overall church ministry. J. Herbert Hinkle says that "far too many of our people think that being a deacon or a choir member is the biggest job in the church. People should constantly be reminded that the greatest job in the New Testament Church is bringing people to Jesus Christ."[153] Each church office or ministry role is a specific responsibility to promote the collective mission of the church - evangelism.

Corporate Worship Service

Included in the overall worship experience is the corporate worship service which takes place at many Seventh-day Adventist churches on Saturday mornings at 11:00 AM. Underscoring the theory that if worship is going to contribute to the growth of your church three things must be evident: 1) members can't wait to attend, 2) members are proud to bring their friends, and 3) whoever

---

[153]Hinkle, 89.

attends is eager to return,[154] I surmise, "You're not going to baptize people if your members aren't comfortable inviting people to church." Hence, church services promoting evangelism should exemplify excellence and be steadily inspiring, intentional, captivating, and spiritual to facilitate increased attendance, excitement, interest, and anticipation.

Given the divine mandate that from "even until even shall you celebrate my Sabbath" (Lev 23:32), worship should be a celebration. The psalmist adds that we "should serve the Lord with gladness" (Psa 100:2). Ellen White says, "The scenes of Calvary call for the deepest emotion. Upon this subject you will be excusable if you manifest enthusiasm."[155] She further states that "our services should be intensely interesting"[156] and that we should "not sing funeral hymns."[157]

Enthusiasm coupled with "seeker-sensitivity," then, should also be resonant in the corporate worship service. This philosophy is echoed in a statement by Julia Duin, "What attracts many baby boomers to the 'good news' of salvation through Jesus are

---

[154]Gladden, *Seven Habits of Highly Ineffective Churches*, 81.

[155]White, *Testimonies*, Vol 2, 213.

[156]Ibid, *Testimonies*, Vol 9, 233.

[157]Ibid, *Evangelism*, 122.

programs that emphasize personal experience, egalitarianism, and dress-down informality."[158] With this in mind, the church needs to be highly participatory and allow individuals to express themselves through involvement and action while in a relaxed, unceremonious, and non-threatening environment. Again, if lively, enthusiastic music, audio-visual materials, dynamic preaching, and special, keen interest shown towards visitors and members during the evangelistic "tent efforts" and other evangelistic campaigns were profitable in "seeking" souls, then why not a reminiscent flavor, reflecting the same message and contextualized in current culture, be profitable in the corporate worship service?

To facilitate this "flavor," some suggestions for the corporate worship service in our postmodern context are as follows:

- Avoid the conventional practice of worship participants (including elders) sitting on the platform, and have them proceed to the platform at their appointed time in the liturgy of the service.
- Make physical plant adjustments including the installation of contemporary pulpit furniture, including acrylic (or glass) lecterns and communion tables to promote equality and intimacy among all in attendance, along with

---

[158]Duin, A-1.

installation of screens for media and technical presentations.

- Avoid making church announcements during the worship service, but have them verbally offered or shown on power point screens for worshipers to view earlier in the worship experience (prior to the worship service).
- Alternate the use of the recitation of the fourth commandment by using a monthly thematic text.
- The welcome period should be highly participatory (personal greetings through shaking hands, greeting neighboring pew congregants, etc.), but the anonymity of visitors should be respected, a desire of most visiting baby boomer, Generation X-ers, Generation Y-ers, and the "Net Generation," as to avoid requesting them to stand at the call of their name.
- Institute a Praise and Worship period affording diversity in song selection and the promotion of congregational participation with singing of "praise and worship" choruses (and hymns) not solely led by a chorister, but rather by a group of singers who engage the congregation in worship. "Your style of music will define who attends your church. In established churches, the natural tendency is to do music to please the older generation. Which likely explains two things. First, why unchurched guests are rare in Adventist

churches. Second, why the average age in the United States is thirty-five while the average Adventist is fifty-three. We have kept our hymnals, but lost our children."[159]

- Employ several instruments in the worship service of congregational singing as opposed to just using the traditional organ and/or piano.
- Promote excellence in the worship service and in musical offerings. The Bible says, "Make a joyful (not awful) noise unto the Lord." Utilize competent, skilled musicians and engage in weekly rehearsals (worship, choir, praise team, musicians, elders, platform participants, etc.). If such skilled musicians are not members in your local congregation, other God- fearing, Christian individuals should be employed to handle this most important position in a professional manner (1 Chr 25 and 1 Sam 14-23).
- Utilize power point on large screens for viewing of "praise and worship" choruses, hymns, scripture readings, etc.
- Streamline service time, utilizing the necessary liturgical elements for worship. The service should succinctly and competently embody the three P's - " Praise, Pray, and Preach."

---

[159] Gladden, *Seven Habits of Highly Ineffective Churches*, 92.

- Adopt a Children's Church Ministry to attractively and relevantly reach children.

A suggested order of worship promoting participation and continuous "flow" in our postmodern culture would be:

- Call to Worship/Invocation
- Congregational Welcome
- Congregational Praise & Worship (and/or Hymn) Singing
- Intercessory Prayer
- Offertory
- Scripture
- Musical Selection(s)
- Sermon
- Appeal
- Benediction

Please note that the aforementioned are suggestions, and should be used and/or adopted to best fit one's ministerial context.

Worship Leadership

The local church pastor is the primary worship leader for the entire worship experience. He/She particularly sets the tone for worship during the actual worship service. The barometer for the energy level of the worship experience is dictated by the verbal and non-verbal actions (words, facial expressions, body language, worship engagement) of the pastor. Hence, it is important that both pastor and church membership are cognizant of this, as the pastor seeks to promote positive worship leadership through word and action.

Although not the primary worship leader, choir members, musicians, elders, ushers, church officers, etc., do bear some leadership responsibility in the worship experience. They, too, must recognize the importance of positive worship participation and engagement. Because congregants, including visitors, observe the behavior of worship participants and local church lay leaders and officers, church members who serve in worship capacities should be mindful of the impact and influence they possess in the worship experience. Active singing, responsive reading, positive interaction, warm fellowship, and worship attention should characterize worship participants.

Given the pastor's role as primary worship leader of the church, the direction and management of worship planning should be reflected in this leadership as well. Encompassing this worship planning is the setting of the comprehensive church calendar to promote evangelism as primarily prepared by the pastor in collaboration with church leaders. Thematic, pastoral worship planning fosters cohesion and continuity. In this calendar preparation, the reduction of inundated "annual" departmental days should be considered as to promote consistency and stability in worship. Typical departmental days have a tendency to encourage an internal as opposed to external focus – evidenced by increased worship service time, emphasis on internal member recognition, and inconsistency in worship service participants.

Hinkle vehemently asserts that "the church must change its calendar to become a soul-winning church."[160] Too often departmental ministries of the church are encumbered with planning and organizing annual "days," and we lose the underlying purpose of our existence which is to promote church growth through effective application of the department's ministry. So rather than consuming the church calendar with Community Service Day, Usher Day, Deacons' Day, Deaconess Day, etc. during the worship service, I would like to offer that these special days should be reduced to days representing demographics (Youth, Seniors, etc.), and emphasize church departmental ministries in Adventist Youth Society (AYS) services, Mid-week services, Sabbath School, and Personal Ministries.

An additional feature that could be added in the annual calendar for the worship experience in harmony with the Seventh-

---

[160]Hinkle, 90.

day Adventist mission of evangelism would be "Praise Sabbaths." These Sabbath celebrations could be held monthly where on this special Sabbath, guest speakers and/or guest choirs share their respective ministries with the church in worship. The guest speakers should be Seventh-day Adventist ministers who resonate with the primacy of evangelism in the local church, and condone the enthusiastic, "seeker-sensitive" flavor being advocated. The special music for "Praise Sabbaths" could be offered by Seventh-day Adventist as well as properly screened non Seventh-day Adventist choirs and groups from the neighboring community. The latter would afford and promote positive community relations with other Christian churches in the area and create a greater awareness of the ministry of the local Seventh-day Adventist Church with the goal of eliciting increased attendance among non Seventh-day Adventist visitors at the weekly worship experience.

Outreach

In harmony with a church's pledge to be evangelistic and "seeker-sensitive" in the worship experience, the church should also be a place where individuals who are seeking God, or even seeking for something better in their lives, find it within the outreach ministries and services of the local church. Hence, community outreach is extremely vital to creating an evangelistic culture at the local church. Nevertheless, outreach ministry identification can no longer be internal, but rather external, in meeting the needs of community residents as opposed to solely the views of Seventh-day Adventists. In short, we have to "scratch where the people are itching." Ellen White says, "He who seeks to understand humanity must himself understand humanity."[161]

Historically, the Seventh-day Adventist Church has been very active in the community through outreach initiatives as previously shared in this book. Yet, there is a need to engage in relevant outreach activities in our postmodern context. Some applicable outreach suggestions for contemporary society include, but are not limited to:

- Musical Programs/Concerts
- Block Parties
- Tract Attacks
- Oil Change Ministry
- Bible Workers
- Marketing – Television, Radio, Billboards, Internet

Musical Programs/Concerts

The love of music is evident in our culture given its widespread popularity among all ages, particularly young people,

---

[161] White, *Education*, 78.

as reflected in fashion, fads, entertainment, recreation, etc. Capitalizing on this popularity, musical programs and concerts provide a tremendous opportunity to attract visitors to the local church. While this is not a necessarily new concept, the contemporary approach to this notion is the utilization of nationally known musical artists whose widespread appeal reaches beyond the sphere of Seventh-day Adventists and greatly influences the masses in the community.

Whether it be special music for the corporate worship service or the opening night of an evangelistic initiative, the probability of numerous visitors attending the local church given the reputation of the musical artist within the community, and his/her accompanying presence, is great. Visitors would then be exposed to the local church, and prayerfully, with a positive experience, they would return for subsequent worship experiences. Furthermore, to create a database of community visitors, which was similar to the purpose of the nightly quiz used in the evangelistic tent effort, special "registration" cards could be distributed to all in attendance at the musical concert/program securing necessary demographic information for future invitations to be sent to guests inviting them to ensuing services, programs, and events, soliciting Bible studies, along with thanking them for worshipping at the local church.

Block Parties

The gospel commission says, "Go ye therefore and teach all nations" (Matt 28:19), it does not say that people will necessarily "come to you." Hence, it is imperative that the local church actively goes in the community and reach people. The Block Party is an innovative initiative which accomplishes this as the church goes directly into the community to minister to neighboring residents.

Held on Sabbath afternoon immediately following the Divine Worship Experience in a civic housing facility located within the neighboring community of the local church, this contemporary outreach initiative consists of a worship program (welcome, music, prayer, brief inspirational thought, Pathfinder drum corps participation, etc.) intentionally planned to appeal to the targeted population and also encompasses the serving of food, distributing clothes, household gifts, and brochures about the local church, all in an informal, festive setting. Like the aforementioned musical programs/concerts, registration cards are distributed to attendees securing necessary demographic information for future program invitations.

Tract Attacks

Immediately following the Divine Worship Experience at 11:00 AM, "Tract Attack" is a soul winning activity where all members of the church collectively go in the neighboring community soliciting Bible studies, having prayer with residents, leaving a brochure about the ministries and services of the church, and inviting residents to church services. Following "Tract Attack," the membership returns to the church for brief testimonies, prayer, and a light meal.

While this is not necessarily a new activity, the name of this initiative, "Tract Attack" is catchy and more attractive than mere references to "going out in the community." Furthermore, this initiative is beneficial to the individual member, the collective church, and the visited resident. The individual member is directly and actively involved in evangelism, the church receives increased publicity and community awareness while gaining new Bible study interests, and the resident is spiritually and socially blessed from the visit.

Oil Change Ministry

This evangelistic initiative is best described by its name, "oil change ministry." On a Sunday, the Deacon Board or Men's Ministries Department, offers free oil change services for neighboring community residents. As individuals seize the opportunity to have this systematic maintenance performed on their automobiles, it creates a positive impression for residents, allows the church membership to interact socially with "oil change" recipients, and like the three previously mentioned outreach suggestions, helps create a database of interest names enabling the church to invite individuals to subsequent church activities.

Bible Workers

The employment of Bible Workers to canvass community residents for Bible studies is a traditional evangelistic practice of the Seventh-day Adventist Church. Historically, however, this employment has primarily been adopted during periods of seasonal public evangelism. When Bible Workers who were employed by the local conference and assigned to local churches on an annual basis were utilized, it was primarily at larger churches with only a few churches in the conference being privileged to have this staff position. Moreover, as we have moved further into the twenty-first century, the number of full time Bible Workers has decreased greatly.

Nevertheless, if the employment of Bible Workers during seasonal public evangelistic campaigns was successful in leading individuals to Jesus Christ and their corresponding baptism, why not employ the same practice in the ministry of the church throughout the calendar year as opposed to a three-month season? During these evangelistic campaigns that were seeker oriented, competent Bible Workers were all gainfully employed to share in the responsibility of public, seasonal evangelism. The salaried Bible Workers were responsible for the home visitation of visitors, greeting all attendees at public evangelistic events, and the teaching of the Bible. While the local pastor, elders, deacons, deaconesses, and members primarily participated in membership visitation, Bible Workers fully focused their attentions on community visitation.

Given the proven impact of Bible Workers to successful evangelism, the priority of their employment should rank very high when creating a church budget for the entire year. Both conference and church alike need to place primacy on the hiring of Bible Workers for the local church. After employing such individuals, Bible Workers should be given the responsibility of "door to door" evangelism by daily knocking on community residents' doors, introducing themselves, soliciting prayer requests, offering Bible studies, and inviting individuals to the worship experience of the local church with goal of seeing persons baptized into the Seventh-day Adventist Church. After these community residents are baptized, the Bible Worker should still visit these individuals and offer ongoing Bible studies, counseling, and support in order to further indoctrinate them and retain their membership and presence within the church.

Marketing – Television, Radio, Print Media, Billboards, and Internet

Another outreach suggestion to help foster an evangelistic culture at the local church is the utilization of marketing through different media including television, radio, billboards, and the internet. The employment of media provides excellent opportunities to increase the awareness of the local church and to inform community residents of the church's ministries. This church exposure and publicity through visible means are essential and necessary to church growth. Callahan suggests that there are three primary areas in which a church must be visible to initiate this growth–"develop the geographical visibility of its site, community visibility with regard to its pastor, key leaders, and major programs, and media visibility in the communications networks that exist in its community."[162] For the sake of this book, let's look at the latter two areas of community visibility.

First, the community needs to have high visibility of the pastor, ministries, and programs of the church. A portion of this visibility is achieved through the implementation of the aforementioned outreach initiatives of the church, coupled with the employment of full time Bible Instructors, and their direct

---

[162]Callahan, 78.

community interaction. This visibility facilitates for positive, informal discussions among church members and community residents regarding the activity and outreach ministries of the church. Further, I truly believe that the greatest advertisement for a church is through the membership.

Another method to promote community visibility of the church is through the utilization of high quality brochures which can include a photograph of the pastor and church building, along with information regarding the church's worship schedule and accompanying ministries. Ironically, in Adventist public evangelistic campaigns, a similar approach is used through the distribution of handbills and flyers promoting the evangelistic initiative and attendance of community residents. Distribution of colorful church brochures throughout the community on a daily basis increases public awareness and visibility of the church akin to the process used in traditional, seasonal Adventist evangelistic campaigns.

Secondly, there needs to be media visibility for the church. "Whether it be newspapers, radio, television, or other forms of media, the extent to which a local church advances its visibility through the media that are available, is the extent to which that local congregation contributes to high visibility."[163] In major

---

[163] Ibid., 81.

American cities, the opportunities for media ministry are endless. Furthermore, the moral decline of our society often hinders "door to door" evangelism in certain neighborhoods. Therefore, the importance of media ministry cannot be devalued and should be implemented to create mass public awareness of the church. Television, radio, print media, billboards, the internet, and other forms of media are able to penetrate homes where individuals cannot. Of particular note is the use of the internet. Given its popularity, accessibility, and inexpensive nature, the internet is an excellent tool to reach community residents through the church's website, streaming worship services, eNewsletters, blogs, *eInvite, myspace, facebook, youtube, craig's list*, etc. Hence, I would highly recommend the use of the internet to promote the church's evangelistic ministry among individuals in our postmodern society.

CHAPTER 7

SUMMARY AND CONCLUSION

The recent regression in the number of per capita baptisms for the Seventh-day Adventist Church in North America suggests that there is an immediate need to combat this declivity with progressive, relevant evangelistic methods to reach our postmodern society. This call is further heightened when this necessity is conjoined with our urgency to reach individuals in our urban areas.

Given our postmodern society, the call to evangelism and church growth is imperative. The coming of Jesus is imminent, and the eschatological overtones in our world are loud and clear. In Matthew 24:6-8, Jesus says, "And ye shall hear of wars and rumors of wars: see that ye be not troubled: for all these things must come to pass, but the end is not yet. For nation shall rise against nation, and kingdom against kingdom: and there shall be famines, pestilences, and earthquakes, in divers places. All these are the beginning of sorrow."

Jesus continues, "And this gospel of the kingdom shall be preached in all the world for a witness unto all nations; and then shall the end come" (Matt 24:14). This pronouncement should motivate our urgency to proclaim the gospel to humanity by the most effective means possible. Complacent, mediocre methods will not suffice. If a player gets to first base in baseball, that's nice, but that's not the objective. The player must get to home plate. If we reach some people with the Seventh-day Adventist message, that's nice, but that's not the objective. The objective is to reach all people. Remember, "the Lord has never told us that the whole world will accept Him, (but) He did definitely commission us to proclaim the gospel to every person on earth."[164] Revelation 14:6-8 says, "And I saw another angel fly in the midst of heaven, having the everlasting gospel to preach unto them that dwell on the earth, and to every nation, and kindred, and tongue, and people, saying with a loud voice, 'Fear God, and give glory to Him; for the hour of His judgment is come: and worship Him that made heaven, and earth, and the sea, and the fountains of waters.'"

The three angels' message of Revelation 14 demands a short chronology prior to Christ's return, not a long one. Because Seventh-day Adventists have an urgent message of the everlasting gospel for the end of time, we must be heard by the maximum number of people before it's too late.[165] For too long we've expected only nominal church growth results in the Seventh-day

---

[164]Gottfried Oosterwal as cited in George E. Knowles, 44.

[165]Gladden, "Building a Home Depot" *Mission Catalyst Network*, 2001, 9.

Adventist Church, but in the perilous days in which we live, we must be progressive, intentional, and insistent about church growth. If we are not, the future of the Seventh-day Adventist Church could resemble the larger, established Christian community, characteristic of decline, dissipation, and ultimately, death.

Although it requires change, the adoption of new, contemporary methods for evangelism is necessary. Change is never easy, but change that is beneficial to the hastening of the second advent of Christ should be espoused and implemented. Kevin Cosby writes, "It has been noted that the gospel has a dual responsibility: 'afflicting the comfortable and comforting the afflicted.' Afflicting the comfortable occurs when Christ disrupts our world and shakes us from our tranquil complacency, self-contentment, and self-satisfaction. Comforting the afflicted happens when Christ gives assurance, solace, and strength to the world's hurting in order to help them move forward toward wholeness."[166]

Changing our methodologies of evangelism to effectively reach contemporary society will "afflict the comfortable" within the Seventh-day Adventist Church. Yet, in so doing, the afflicted, those who have not heard this precious Seventh-day Adventist

---

[166]Kevin W. Cosby, *Get Off Your But!* (Lithonia, GA: Orman Press, 2000), 10.

message, will be comforted. If "seeker-sensitive" elements incorporated in the worship experience, intentional hospitality, impacting outreach ministries, and streamlined bureaucracy are all typical of current growing churches in American Christianity, and resemble the components of "tent efforts" and other public evangelistic campaigns in former years when the Seventh-day Adventist Church was "seeking" souls, then why wouldn't a reminiscent flavor applicable for our contemporary age be profitable?

Therefore, I would like to recommend that the evangelistic program as outlined in Chapter 6 of this project, inclusive of its design and implementation, be adopted to promote the increased number of baptisms in the Seventh-day Adventist Church in North America. The specific suggestions and strategies as outlined are proven methods and practices that elicit church growth.

Furthermore, I do not believe that North American Seventh-day Adventists should fear or become apprehensive regarding the employment of these contemporary evangelism recommendations due to unpopularity, traditions, finances, etc. Although the process by which these suggestions are implemented will vary based on the cultural environs of the respective community and church, their employment is critical to the continued vitality and growth of the Seventh-day Adventist Church. The primary function for the church's existence is rooted in evangelism, and therefore, all resources should correspond to this priority.

To everything there is a time and season (Ecclesiastes 3), and as we progress through the twenty-first century, it should be remembered that we must preach and teach the same Seventh-day Adventist message, yet with new, different methodologies. The same God who led the Seventh-day Adventist Church in the past will continue to lead the church in the future. "We have nothing to fear for the future, except as we shall forget the way the Lord has led us, and His teaching in our past history."[167]

Consider the words of Charles Scriven:

There has arisen this wariness of the "new" in theology, this feeling that our proper business today is merely to perpetuate and combat the errors of those who disagree with us. We have interpreted Jesus' promise to the disciples to have a cut-off point, as though the Spirit of truth lies buried in the cemeteries of New England and Battle Creek. Perhaps we ourselves are endangered by the doctrine that God is dead: for in this we say, or seem to say that God has no new thing to teach us, then we come seriously close to making Him a fallen hero. Fortunately, a fresh reading of Scripture – as well as of Ellen White, who

---

[167] Ellen G. White, *Christian Experience and Teachings of Ellen G. White* (Washington, DC: Review and Herald Publishing Association, 1922), 204.

envisioned the unfolding of "new truth" through all eternity – can give us strength against the temptation of skepticism. Indeed, it can provide us resources upon which to base a positive renaissance of theological creativity in the church.[168]

Isaiah 48:6 says, "Thou hast heard, see all this; and will not ye declare it? I have shewed thee new things from this time, even hidden things, and thou didst not know them." If we just seek God first, and His righteousness, then all these things shall be added unto us (Matt 6:33).

---

[168]Charles Scriven, "The Case for Renewal in Adventist Theology," *Spectrum*, 8, no. 1 (September 1976): 4.